DE-INTEGRATE!

MAX CZOLLEK

DE-INTEGRATE!

A Jewish Survival Guide for the 21st Century

Translated from the German
by Jon Cho-Polizzi

RESTLESS BOOKS
BROOKLYN, NEW YORK

First Restless Books hardcover edition January 2023

Hardcover ISBN: 9781632063182
Library of Congress Control Number: 2022943003

This work is published with support from David Bruce Smith,
Grateful American Foundation.

Cover design by Alex Robbins
Set in Garibaldi by Tetragon, London

Printed in the United States

1 3 5 7 9 10 8 6 4 2

Restless Books, Inc.
232 3rd Street, Suite A101
Brooklyn, NY 11215

restlessbooks.org
publisher@restlessbooks.org

CONTENTS

Introduction: De-Integrate Yourselves!   vii

1 The Theater of Memory: Staged Remembrance   3
2 Normality Reloaded: Schlaaaaand   21
3 The Early Years: Integrating Nazis   34
4 The Theater of Integration! *Leitkultur* and Ministries
     of *Heimat*   54
5 That German Desire: On the Function of the Jews   70
6 Wowschwitz, or: Can We Laugh about Auschwitz?   88
7 Alternatives for Germans: What We Can Learn from
     the AfD   104
8 "No Integration": De-Integration and Its Progenitors 121
9 Like They Do in Babylon: On Jewish Diversity   140
10 Inglourious Poets: Revenge as Self-Empowerment   157
11 Ahasver's Hell: Or, Things Will Never Be "All Good"
     Again   177
12 The Beginning Is Nigh: *DE-INTEGRATSIЯ*   188

Acknowledgments   201
Bibliography   203
About the Author and Translator   217

INTRODUCTION

DE-INTEGRATE YOURSELVES!

THE BOOK YOU HOLD in your hands is not a moving biographical account. It's not about the history of my family—about how a part of it was murdered—nor is it about the miraculous survival of my Communist, Jewish grandfather and the lives of his wife and children in the German Democratic Republic (East Germany). This book is not about my own experiences with antisemitism any more than it is about my relationship to Israel. Because you all already know these stories. You can read about them in books, watch them at the cinema, hear about them at a klezmer concert, or experience them at the theater. You may not realize it, but you already know *everything* about Jewish literature, Jewish music, Jewish biographies. In case you've forgotten, you just need to look it up.

This book will proceed differently. Instead, I will attempt to analyze the German image of the Jews and ask: What—if anything—do living Jewish people have to do with this picture? This can be entertaining at times, and at other times depressing. I believe that the official representation of the Jews in Germany reveals much more about German society's own self-conception than it does about Jewish people. Since Reunification, German society has developed an increasing aspiration for "normality." *Is* everything back to normal again? Given recent political developments, this notion has become even more suspect than it already was. The AfD, PEGIDA, NSU:* There is little in Germany that I regard as normal. And this lack of normality is manifest as much in the awkward relationship between Jews and Germans today as it is—more fundamentally—in the way the concept of "belonging" gets discussed in this part of the world. The book you hold in your hands concerns these things.

And so, dear readers, when I bid you to "de-integrate yourselves!" I'm also trying to problematize those supposedly "positive" forms of nationalism that lurk behind concepts like German *Leitkultur* [guiding culture],† a "Judeo-Christian

---

* Alternative für Deutschland [Alternative for Germany] (an increasingly successful far-right political party with seats in the Bundestag); Patriotische Europäer gegen die Islamisierung des Abendlandes [Patriotic Europeans Against the Islamization of the Occident] (a far-right political movement founded in Dresden); Nationalsozialistischer Untergrund [National Socialist Underground] (a neo-Nazi terrorist organization responsible for a series of high-profile murders and other crimes in the late 1990s and early 2000s). [N.B. All footnotes are the translator's.]

† *Leitkultur* signifies the hegemony or 'guiding culture' of the dominant social group—one of the central components in the integration narrative.

West," or the recent founding of a German Heimatministerium [Ministry of Homeland].* I offer my critique of these concepts from a Jewish perspective. And this perspective also includes analyses of Germany's changing self-image over the past decades. Because if we're going to talk about Jews living in Germany today, we cannot keep quiet about the Germans in Germany.

Who is considered Jewish in Germany today? Someone with a Jewish mother? Someone who can exhibit their Jewish biography? Someone who can tell good jokes? Someone with relatives in Israel? Someone who eats bone-dry, unleavened bread for a week instead of Easter eggs? Someone who has read all the Philip Roth novels, watched all the seasons of *Seinfeld*, or hung a poster of the Jewish rapper Drake in their bedroom? Is a person Jewish because they are neurotic, or neurotic because they are a Jew? Because their own family was in Auschwitz? Because they can't help but want to sleep with blonde people? Or because blonde people can't help but want to sleep with them? Is a person Jewish because they want

---

* *Heimat* is a contested and politically loaded term for 'homeland' (among other things, associated with National Socialist ambitions for expansion, nostalgia for the 'lost' formerly German-speaking territories in Central and Eastern Europe, and deeply intertwined with the fantasy of an ethnically and politically homogeneous nation or *Volk*). Because this term is highly culturally specific within a German-language context, it is frequently left untranslated in the remaining text: i.e., Ministry of *Heimat*.

to smash Nazis' heads in? Or is a person Jewish because they have to think about what it means to be a Jew?

Just who comes to be considered Jewish in Germany is not something Jewish people themselves decide upon alone. It's not about one's own cultural or intellectual positionality: one's personal relationship to religion, ethnicity, or history. "The Jews" today are figures on the stage of Germany's Theater of Memory—a concept introduced by Berlin sociologist Y. Michal Bodemann in his 1996 work *Gedächtnistheater. Die jüdische Gemeinschaft und ihre deutsche Erfindung* [Theater of Memory: The Jewish Community and its German Invention]. Bodemann employs this term to describe those well-trodden interactions between German society and its Jewish minorities—the Jewish role in a script titled *The Good Germans*. Because for decades now, the public role of Jews has existed to affirm the *German Redemption Story*.

In 2016, there were approximately 100,000 official, registered members of Jewish congregations living in Germany. If I were to increase this number to include those Jewish people who are not official members of Jewish congregations, the number would double to about 200,000. With a total of 82.5 million inhabitants, that's approximately 0.24 percent of Germany's population. Some of these people were born in Germany. Others come from Russia or Eastern Europe, Israel, Yemen, Ethiopia, Iraq, France, or the United States. Many of my Jewish friends have moved to Germany over the last few years from all over the world. Some of them have no personal connection to the Shoah. Thank God. And not all of them know how to play the clarinet. Or fiddle. Instead, they bring stories with them to Germany that do not necessarily correspond to the expectations of the Jewish (and non-Jewish) public here. The resulting diversity of Jewish (hi)stories can hardly compete with Germany's perpetually high demand for very particular Jewish characters. None of us were prepared for this diversity. And this includes the Jewish institutions in Germany, which have only reluctantly begun to reflect upon or actively seek to change their roles in the German Theater of Memory.

The Theater of Memory creates a demand for specific Jewish figures who can reaffirm the assumption that German society has successfully processed and overcome its murderous past. One result of this demand is that the public visibility of Germany's relatively few Jewish inhabitants is at once conspicuously high and strikingly limited. There are other groups who also experience a similarly heavy burden of dominant social expectations. Muslims, for example, are permanently relegated in the public eye to making commentary on gender roles, terrorism, and integration; in doing so, they provide a foil for Germany's own self-conception as a nation of tolerant and enlightened human beings. In both cases, minority roles are interrogated from an unnamed position of power that remains conveniently invisible. I designate this dominant positionality as—*Achtung!*—German. In doing so, I by no means wish to imply that Jewish or Muslim people are not German citizens. Quite the opposite: Their disparate communities represent one of the few glimmers of hope for Germany. Yet the social attribution of roles in this country has had the consequence that many perspectives and experiences are disregarded the very moment they cease to comply with German expectations. And as long as there remains no Central Council of Germans[*] to immediately distance itself from terror attacks committed by German terrorists, the markers "Jews," "Muslims," and "Germans" remain indispensable to a critical reflection on the asymmetrical speakers' positions of these social groups. This book concentrates, primarily, on the juxtaposition of Germans and Jews.

In questioning the function of Jewish people in Germany over the following pages, I also want to give the snow globe of Germany's self-image a thorough shake. I believe that Germans have fundamentally misunderstood their responsibility for the past in their decades-long fantasy pursuit of a new normality.

---

[*]   Zentralrat der Deutschen, a play on the title of the organizations Zentralrat der Muslime in Deutschland / Zentralrat der Juden in Deutschland [Central Council of Muslims / Jews in Germany] and the expectation that these will speak for their corresponding communities in relation to conflicts with broader German society.

This became conspicuous, *at the very latest*, with the election of AfD-representatives to the German Bundestag.* But I think one could draw a line from the black-red-and-gold excesses of the 2006 World Cup to the federal elections of 2017 that, of course, doesn't correspond to the prevailing interpretations. At the time, German feuilletons celebrated the World Cup as an expression of positive nationalism, a new German lightness-of-being. Even today, people are loath to abandon this proud patting of one's own self on the back. This new nationalism was further underscored with the establishment of a government Ministry of *Heimat*. Today, elected representatives in Germany are once again publicly prioritizing their support of *das deutsche Volk*, and in doing so, deliberately excluding those people with German passports but the wrong religious faith. *This* is normality in Germany.

You may have already noticed: I did not write this book impartially or with the intention of examining these themes from every angle. I do not speak from a neutral position. I speak as a poet, a Berliner, and a Jew. In varying order. The (hi)stories of the descendants of German perpetrators interest me most where they directly impact my own life. But I have no particular empathy for their perspectives, nor do I resonate with calls for sympathy vis-à-vis Germany's stricken sense of national identity. Shortly before Christmas 2017, when the

---

* German parliament—both the building and the political body.

centrist SPD politician Sigmar Gabriel called for a positive reevaluation of German concepts like *Heimat* and guiding culture as a reaction to the electoral gains of the far-right AfD, I did not see this as an act of political pragmatism, but rather as the harbinger of a coming storm. After years of official calm, the winds had shifted back to nationalism—even for big party politics. The AfD is only a sideshow. Its influence is like that of an indicator fluid poured over the spectrum of German politics: Suddenly things everywhere are staining Nazi brown. [*]

Given this situation, I can only imagine two viable courses of action: building bridges of empathy toward the opposing camp, or strengthening and expanding one's own position. At least with this book, I'm not interested in building bridges. When I write about the present state of German-Jewish relations (and so, about the present state of Germany itself), I am concerned above all with honing my (our) intellectual tools. I consider the AfD and its voters my political opponents— opponents whom I take seriously. I do not believe that we have had a misunderstanding, any more than I believe that we have much to say to one another. And this does not make for some banal observation in a time when all of Germany's major political parties are actively courting AfD voters. All

---

[*]   Counterintuitively, given contemporary English-language associations with the word, in the context of German politics (where each political party is associated with a color on electoral maps), being 'brown' is associated with National Socialism.

of a sudden, it seems like everyone thinks it was a mistake not to just come out and reaffirm nationalist concepts.

Of course, my rejection of bridges, red carpets, and friend requests from the new political camps of proud and *Heimat*-loving Germans doesn't mean that I've avoided engaging with their "thinkers." Quite the contrary. But after reading such rightwing blockbusters as *Metapolitik* by Thor von Waldstein, *Finis Germania* by Rolf Peter Sieferle, and *Mit Linken leben* [Living with Leftists] by Caroline Sommerfeld and Martin Lichtmesz, I've decided to postpone my studies at the Institute for National Policy* for now, despite evidence of its increasing popularity as an investigative field destination for the German mass media.

Which is to say: I also think that it's important to study one's political opponents before making jokes about them. First of all, because these jokes are more fulfilling when you work hard for them. Secondly, an intervention grows more precise the better one knows one's enemy. But still, I have to admit: These readings were far from pleasurable. After ordering the aforementioned books, Google's algorithm immediately prompted me with links to *Wehrmacht* accessories

---

* Institut für Staatspolitik (IfS): Founded in 2000, a private institution and thinktank considered to be a driving force behind the intellectual and ideological developments of Germany's New Right.

from the supermarket EDEKA, links to Donald Trump's campaign speeches, and an invitation for a romantic spa night in Brandenburg—clinking crystal on *Kristallnacht* (cohabitants or partners welcome).

In their obnoxious 2017 *Mit Linken leben*, Lichtmesz and Sommerfeld attempt to disguise their problematic political positions under the guise of alleged realism. The Left lies to fabricate itself a better world while the Right "has reason, morality, facts, and realism on [its] side" (21). I would like to counter their assertion with the claim that my own book is far more realistic than *Mit Linken leben*. Say what you will: Our social reality is one of sexual, political, ideological, and physical diversity. And I freely admit that I reject their vision of "ethnic and cultural homogeneity" (194). I want no part in this sociopolitical vision. Try as I might, I see neither a shred of recognition for the lived reality of cultural diversity, nor even an iota of honesty when it comes to realizing the current aims championed by representatives of the New Right. Because given its current state of social diversity, arriving at an ethnically and culturally homogeneous Germany would simply require ethnic and cultural cleansing. If they would just admit to *this* reality, then we could resume our conversation. But that's where it would begin.

And if this point is clear, then it should also be clear that I'm not "accidentally" leaving anybody out. I haven't failed to consider anyone. But those who have swung further to the right over the past years never wanted to ride tandem on my bicycle. And so, if my editor or some other representative from the marketing department at my publishing house feels like inquiring about my target audience, I'd like to put this on record right here in my introduction: This book is for everyone who doesn't want to deny me my existence in this country—or the existence of my friends and our allies. Because the *foundation* of our existence here is a pluralistic and democratic society. We will not surrender this society so easily. And therefore we cannot and will not permit *völkisch*-ethnonationalist[*] thought to dominate the discourse of belonging in Germany.

And so, until further notice, I will be excluding the 12.6 percent of the electorate in the 2017 federal election who voted for the AfD from my target audience. That's why my language isn't about provoking them when I use gender-inclusive pronouns.[†]

---

[*] From the German *Volk*—which is often translated as 'people' or 'nation.' In a specifically German political context, the term *völkisch* could be almost synonymous with the English 'ethnonationalist.' Given the unique specificities of German ethnonationalism in the context of National Socialism, German expressions such as "*völkisch und nationalistisch*" are typically translated here as *völkisch*-ethnonationalist to emphasize the specifically German connotations of this tradition.

[†] The original German makes use of the -*innen suffix as a gender-inclusive plural form for all people-related nouns. The author highlights this alleged 'provocation' of the Right here through his use of gender-inclusive grammar.

In doing so, I simply attempt to acknowledge the reality that there are more than two gender identities—a fact that has, by the way, been affirmed by Germany's Constitutional Court since 2017. My terminology for describing the Jewish agents in my text follows its own logic, as well.* Whenever possible, I use the words "Jewish people" in reference to the plurality of identities represented across the contemporary Jewish world. I use the terms "Jews" or—more often than not—"the Jews" when I wish to draw attention to the specific role ascribed to those actors in the German Theater of Memory. The idea behind this is simple: Jewishness and Judaism—in Germany, just like elsewhere in the world—are composed of different, concrete Jewish people. The Theater of Memory, on the other hand, employs only the Germans vis-à-vis the Jews.

The central concept of this book is de-integration. It should be obvious from the word itself that *de*-integration is a response to Germany's constant political and cultural demand for *integration* among its many minoritized communities. However, I do not direct my concept of de-integration solely in support of those individuals addressed in Germany variously as Turks, asylum seekers, North Africans, Muslims, economic refugees, migrants, or Jews. When I write about

---

*   Here the original German also describes the complications of using the -*innen suffix with the existing German plural noun(s) for Jews (*Juden/ Jüdinnen*) due to the gendered vowel shift in the root word.

integration concepts or integration paradigms, I mean the larger construct of a cultural and political "center" that implicitly or explicitly conceptualizes itself as German. I argue that thinking in categories such as integration or guiding culture not only fails to prevent fantasies of ethnic homogeneity and cultural dominance, it also shares responsibility for the fact that these ideas haven't remained on the trash heaps of history where they belong. With the concept of de-integration, I propose a societal model that would render such *neovölkisch* fantasies as impossible as they are implausible.

At the same time, the program of de-integration targets both a Jewish as well as an all-encompassing societal concern: the way in which Jewish people are employed in the German Theater of Memory—and the insight that this Theater cannot be overcome without a fundamental critique of concepts of integration. This conundrum poses quite a falafel, even when viewed from the opposite perspective. Because every concept of integration necessitates the claim of a "center" that no longer corresponds to the social reality in which I or my friends live today. The break from reality that such an integration paradigm demands becomes particularly evident in the ongoing fuss about an alleged "German guiding culture." And this phantasm is currently upheld in Germany through the pretense of a supposed "Judeo-Christian" tradition coupled with an exhaustive discussion of the mass murder of Jewish people during the Second World War. And so, the acute correlation between Germany's self-conception and Germany's Jews renders the Theater of Memory a uniquely appropriate starting point for a critique of Germany's concepts of integration.

Writing this book, I sometimes felt like that elderly Polish woman who—in 2017—held up a sign that read: "I can't believe I still have to protest this fucking shit" during a demonstration for the right to access safe abortion services. Thirty years after the end of the Cold War, which divided Germany into two unequal halves, two sides are again staring each other down across a no-man's-land. But instead of an "antifascist" socialism against a "free" and Western capitalism, it's now actual societal diversity against a conservative revolution. *Völkisch*-ethnonationalist thought is back in the political mainstream. Sometimes I think I'm losing it. Or I despair. And here, dear reader, you see a bit of how I work: lamentation and writing are two facets of my authorial existence.

This is a book by someone who did not set out to become a Jew, but rather a political scientist, an author, an intellectual. And a book by someone who, in the end, became a Jew, as well. Someone who received his doctorate from the Center for Research on Antisemitism. Someone who forged new alliances to counteract the role assigned to him as a Jewish writer. Someone who co-organized the De-Integration Congress in 2016 and the Radical Jewish Cultural Days in 2017 at the

Maxim Gorki Theater in Berlin, in order to conceptualize new strategies for dealing with the role expectations of a German public. Please note that you will not find out much about my own life in this book. I'm not doing this to annoy you. I'm doing it because biographical confession is the active capital of every minoritized individual. It is the fuel of "migrant," "Jewish," "queer," or "feminist" art whose contents are first tapped, then refined, and finally consumed by a greedy public.

Alas, my book is not an oil field. Its pages are not available for representational fracking. It is, instead, my contribution to one of the most important social debates of the coming years—and it makes tangible suggestions for how one might position oneself in this debate. Rules of thumb, if you will. Or maybe rules of fist.

DE-INTEGRATE!

1

THE THEATER OF MEMORY: STAGED REMEMBRANCE

A FEW SUMMERS AGO, my friends and I organized a movie night on a flat rooftop in the southeast of Berlin. Popcorn in one hand, beer in the other, we sat on the tarpaper roof watching *I Am Not Your Negro*, a film about the (US-)American philosopher and activist James Baldwin. In recent years, I've come to appreciate Baldwin, despite the peculiar things he's said about Jews. I am impressed by the composure with which he manages to bring issues to a point before allowing their consequences to fall suddenly like a hammer blow. Just take the following quote by way of example: "History is not the past. It is the present. We carry our history with us. We are our history."

I can think of a German equivalent for this passage—the opening lines to the novel *Kindheitsmuster* [Patterns of Childhood] by Christa Wolf: "The past is *not dead*; it isn't even past. We separate ourselves from it, and feel estranged" (9). Both authors underscore the central role that our histories play. Both claim that the past continues to operate on the present, even if we refuse to admit it. And both warn of the consequences of rejecting this insight. I resolved then, as I opened another beer, to begin my own book by grappling with German-Jewish history. We clanked bottles, raising a toast. The next afternoon, sitting in front of my laptop beside my second liter of coffee, the problems began in earnest. Because memory—well, remembering—is the Achilles' heel of postwar Germany.

To commemorate the 40th anniversary of the end of World War II in Europe, President Richard von Weizsäcker held a speech in the Bundestag on May 8, 1985, which has become a defining document for the new German perspective on the War. And indeed, to its credit, the speech insists upon reflecting on the responsibility of German society and politics surrounding National Socialism. And this was something new back then. But at the same time, the then President also impressed members of parliament with his claim that the 8th of May represented a day on which the Germans had been "*liberated* from the inhuman system of National Socialist tyranny." His statement is so blatantly untrue that I often ask myself what could have motivated Weizsäcker to say a thing like this. Because the majority of Germans, of course, were not *liberated* on May 8, 1945. They were finally and definitively defeated after supporting the Nazi regime to the bitter end—and still further beyond. National Socialism was, after all, truly a popular movement.

As a legal scholar and historian, Weizsäcker knew exactly what he was saying. And quite obviously, his goal was not to describe historical facts, but rather to define a new way of remembering National Socialism's crimes. He makes this clear over the course of his speech. Following a long list of the groups victimized by Nazi violence, he finally arrives at a discussion of the Jews: assigning them the role of model victim for the atrocities of National Socialism. However, he does not cite inspiration here from Christian tradition to remind Germany of its moral convictions. Rather curiously, he instead quotes a dictum by the celebrated Hasidic rabbi Baal Shem Tov: "Seeking to forget makes exile all the longer; the secret of redemption lies in remembrance."

This was a particularly choice carrot that Weizsäcker dangled in front of the noses of the assembled lawmakers: If *you Germans* remember the extermination of the Jews, you will not only find forgiveness, but salvation. But could this reference to Baal Shem Tov also serve as a kind of kosher stamp whereby one employs Jews—both living and dead—to further a German desire for forgiveness? The answer would, of course, depend on how the speech proceeded. Weizsäcker argues that Germans retain a particular obligation to the Jews because:

> Remembrance means an experience of the work of God in history. It is the source of our faith in redemption. This experience creates hope, it creates faith in redemption, in

reunification of the divided, in reconciliation. Whoever forgets this experience loses his faith.

Are we still talking about the event that some refer to as the "burnt offering" [Greek: *Holocaust*]; the event that Jewish people call *Shoah*, meaning "catastrophe"? Wait, what? Now, I can't speak for how other people see it, but for me, the Shoah is neither a great example of the "experience of the work of God" nor is it a "source of faith in redemption." More like the opposite: The Shoah is the point for me at which belief in God gets complicated. But that was not what Weizsäcker was shooting for; his was a different aim. He continues:

> If we for our part sought to forget what has occurred, instead of remembering it, this would not only be inhuman. We would also impinge upon the faith of the Jews who survived and destroy the basis of reconciliation.

Oh, sure: That's what he means! German cultural memory is an act of humility, enacted so as not to impinge upon the *faith of the Jews*. The extermination of the Jews is then a question of faith? I always thought it was established fact. How convenient that the secret to Jewish salvation happens to be remembering, as well. The Germans can thus resolve two problems in a single load of hogwash: forgiveness *and* salvation. And, as if Weizsäcker really needed to remind the members of the Bundestag just why remembering National Socialism was important, he underscored that one should do so for the Jews' sake.

The whole thing reminds me of a classic Jewish joke: "What is chutzpah?"* "Chutzpah is when a person murders their father and mother, and then pleads mitigating circumstances before the court as a poor orphan."

I think citing "Jewish tradition" as an argument for the imperative of *German* remembrance is a bit misplaced. It's as if Weizsäcker wasn't even concerned with Jewish people. Instead, he wanted to sell Germany a new self-image that would affix its lost War with new, positive connotations. Which is why he describes May 8, 1945, as a day of *liberation* and not as a resounding defeat—which is certainly how most Germans must have experienced it. This also explains why he conjures up Jewish tradition in order to transform the Holocaust memories of a community of perpetrators into something almost sexy: "Liberation by the Allied Forces and salvation through the Jewish victims" sounds so much better than "one hand on the gas valve and Nazi till the bitter end!" With his speech, Weizsäcker aimed at making the remembrance of their own crimes more palatable for German society. And Germans took the bait. And swallowed it so wholeheartedly that only a few decades later—breast swollen with pride—the

---

* Yiddish for audacity or cheekiness, from the Hebrew חֻצְפָּה.

Reunified country proclaimed itself the World Champion of Remembrance.

Weizsäcker's speech is a milestone in the German discovery (and implementation) of exterminated Jews as part of their own self-image. This invention of *Vergangenheitsbewältigung* [coming to terms with the past]* held grave consequences for the *living* Jewish people in Germany—who suddenly found themselves at the center of a German process of self-definition. Jewish sociologist Y. Michal Bodemann devotes his aforementioned 1996 study, *Gedächtnistheater*, to precisely this process, although he had already anticipated its central ideas as early as 1991, in an essay for the journal *Babylon*. In this essay, Bodemann describes how a form of remembrance prevailed in 1980s West German cultural memory by which "Auschwitz and *Kristallnacht* [became] a horror of shared suffering, romanticized and idealized: Jews and the good Germans against the evil societal powers [of National Socialism]" ("Endzeit," 14). By the end of the 1970s, the German state had increasingly come to support Jewish commemorative ceremonies. For Bodemann, this was

---

* *Vergangenheitsbewältigung*: an important concept in the discourse of contemporary German cultural memory; literally, "overcoming the past." This word has several common translations in English (including the aforementioned 'coming to terms with the past'). For later comparisons with the author's own concept of *Gegenwartsbewältigung* [overcoming the present], the translation "overcoming the past" is typically preferred (see Chapter 3).

a decisive step toward the emergence of a German Theater of Memory. In his own words: "Precisely the point at which remembrance was converted to national commemoration required Jews—the dead Jews, as well as the living bodies of Jews" (*Gedächtnistheater*, 118). According to Bodemann, the German Theater of Memory is composed of a combination of three elements. It stages remembrance "as a creative and dramatic act, like that of an act in a theatrical play," in which the German perpetrators and their descendants meet with the good Jewish victims, providing catharsis. The Theater of Memory is also an expression of mourning, "typically depicting a unifying act of extreme violence," which in this case is, of course, the Holocaust or Shoah. Finally, the Theater of Memory fulfills the function "[of a] collective endowment of identity"—namely, the construction of a new self-image for Germans as a reformed and liberated people (183).

Jewish people are undeniably an important element in the German Theater of Memory, but just like in a real theatrical performance, it's not really about the individual persons, but rather, the roles they play. In this case: their symbolic meaning as representatives of those who were exterminated. And this is only logical, because the function of the Theater of Memory is not to represent Jewish plurality, but to redeem the promise of reconciliation for German society. The construction of the German self-image since the 1980s has been substantially informed by a specific, strident, and oft-repeated politics of memory; and this is why the role ascribed to Jews, *the Jewish role*, ultimately serves to stabilize this German self-conception.

A good example of the self-referentiality within the German Theater of Memory was the discussion a few years back around the independent "Experts Group on Antisemitism" appointed by the Bundestag. When these experts reconvened at the end of February 2015, some observers noted with surprise that neither a single one of the six academics nor either of the two representatives from organizations in civil society was Jewish. When confronted with this detail, a speaker from the Federal Ministry of the Interior explained that the expert group had not been staffed according to religious affiliation, but rather, technical expertise. Ah, yes: They just couldn't find a single Jewish expert on antisemitism. I'd like to review this line of argumentation speculatively: The Ministry of the Interior wanted to staff its Experts Group on Antisemitism with experts. Expertise means the ability to judge one's subject matter impartially. The fact that all of the invited experts were non-Jewish, then, suggests the assumption that Jewish people cannot be impartial on the subject of antisemitism. But, according to the Ministry of the Interior, members of a society who within living memory consented to the segregation and extermination of their fellow citizens have a clear, impartial advantage over those whose hair and skin were used for manufacturing purposes. In other words, the Jews are only wanted when Germans can benefit from their utilization.

Of course, the Theater of Memory is more fun when "Jewish dramas and Jewish actors" play along (Bodemann, *Gedächtnistheater*, 99): They simply add a bit more glamor to the whole procedure. But the production of the Theater of Memory can also dispense with living Jews, particularly when they become uncomfortably conspicuous. Razed synagogues can be rebuilt without Jewish carpenters, Jewish museums can be staffed by German curators, and one can also pat oneself on the back and drink prosecco at joint commemorative celebrations even when no Jewish people attend: uptight and unhinged all at once.

From a historical perspective, the positionality of Germany's Jewish population has experienced a remarkable turnaround. In the Christian antisemitism of the nineteenth and twentieth centuries (just like in its leftwing, rightwing, and liberal counterparts), the Jews still occupied their role as the evil or even disgusting murderers of Jesus Christ, greedy capitalists, or Communists. In post-National Socialist Germany, on the other hand, they have been ascribed an entirely new role in which they have ascended to become an integral part of Germany's self-conception. As pure and goodly victims, Jews help stabilize the image of the benevolent, redeemed, and *normal* German. On the following pages, if I seem to privilege the term "Jewish positionality" over "Jewish identity," I do so because I want to suggest that Jewish people have come to fulfill a function as "the Jews for the Germans," which doesn't

11

necessarily correspond with the Jewish portion of their individual identities. Or at least I hope not.

With this, I'd like to return to that warm, flat rooftop in the southeast of Berlin, and to the movie about James Baldwin and its thematization of the United States during the 1950s and 1960s. Baldwin grappled with the white, racist society of his times. In doing so, he came into contact with diverse figures: from Martin Luther King, Jr. to Malcom X. Baldwin describes how both men found themselves in nearly identical public positions, despite representing opposing viewpoints. Because from the dominant, white perspective, the overwhelming differences between King and Malcolm X receded behind their shared positionality as Black men. For mainstream American society, both were simply representatives of the Civil Rights Movement, just as Jewish people in Germany today are automatically part of a "Jewish community" regardless of their individual associations, their political or religious affiliations. In both cases, the differentiated visibility of minoritized groups becomes severely constrained by external role expectations.

I am convinced that one cannot adequately understand the German-Jewish relationship through the sole study of what Jewish people do and where they congregate—even through direct surveys or interviews. Because such inquiries always converge (not coincidentally) around the same topics: antisemitism, the Holocaust, and Israel. And as soon as a

Jewish person responds to a question about one of these themes, they find themself center stage in the Theater of Memory. This works in a similar fashion to what French philosopher Louis Althusser describes with the cry of a policeman to a passerby. The policeman shouts: "Hey, you there!" and as soon as the passerby turns, they have become subject to the state's apparatus of power. An analogous submission to the cry of the Theater of Memory becomes an all but inevitable process if one doesn't wish to abandon discussions of antisemitism, the Holocaust, and Israel from a Jewish perspective completely. And for this reason alone, this book does not concern itself simply with finding a way out of the Theater of Memory, but rather with the latitude Jewish people can attain through understanding these underlying dynamics.

Michal Bodemann's work on the Theater of Memory continues to deliver insight on the functional mechanics of the German present, even now, more than twenty years after its publication. Now, as then, Jewish people continue to operate on a coordinate field determined by the demands of a dominant German positionality. These demands limit the representation of Jewishness to experiences with antisemitism, views on Israel, and potential familial or artistic relations to the Shoah. A smattering of religion and (successfully negotiated) migration history can add a bit of spice, but these do not permit one to operate beyond the prescribed framework. Things haven't always been this way. The relationship between this new German self-image and dead Jews has intensified since the late 1970s. In the process, the extermination of the Jews has increasingly become a codeword for all the other things from which Germans would like to distance themselves. And this led to the present situation, in which Germans primarily know only one thing about the Jews: that they murdered them.

The symbolic power of the Jew becomes particularly strong when it's combined with broader social-political conflict lines. These often have very little to do with Jewish people at first glance. Think, for example, about popular German expressions like "Judeo-Christian culture" or the "Judeo-Christian West." Conservative policymakers use these kinds of descriptors in order to distance their own understanding of German tradition and culture from Islam. Because they can. To claim a shared "Judeo-Christian culture" is, of course, misleading at best: It distorts historical facts beyond all recognition. If there was ever a Judeo-Christian culture in Germany, it was one of the Christian majority appropriating Jewish traditions and writings. Christians rarely gave a damn about the cultural contributions or existential needs of the Jewish people living in their midst. Instead, with considerable regularity, they banished, dispossessed, or murdered them. I would not wish such an Islamic-Christian tradition on any Muslim out there.

Conservative discourse on Judeo-Christian culture has become part of the attempt to exclude Islam from German society—and to tolerate Jewishness for the time being. Even if the short-term effects of this discursive shift are to safeguard the Jewish population from discrimination, I can only warn against participating in this game of divide and conquer. History can deliver helpful lessons when it comes to the temptation of cooperating with the powers that be: Whenever minorities start to be marginalized, Jews have always found themselves on the side of the discriminated-against more quickly than they might wish to admit today. And Jewish and Muslim communities have, in fact, found themselves in the same pressure cooker of populist politics in recent years. From the so-called "circumcision debate"* to discussions about the ritual slaughter of animals. Or have you already forgotten about the public demand for—*Achtung!*—making pork consumption compulsory in Northern German preschools? At the beginning of 2016, several newspapers reported that preschools in Schleswig-Holstein were considering eliminating pork from their menus so that Muslim (and Jewish) children could eat together with their peers. The CDU state government reacted with the campaign: "German children eat their pork where, how, and however

---

* The political discussion in recent years to regulate the circumcision of (male) minors for religious purposes on humanitarian grounds.

much they like." I feel sorry for all the pigs. And for the children.

In the face of such petit-bourgeois incendiaries, I am sorely tempted to counter claims of a Judeo-Christian tradition with those of a Judeo-Muslim hegemony. It would be nice to see Muslim-Jewish cooperation occur outside acute instances of their shared marginalization. Of course, there is a good degree of antisemitism among Muslims, and rampant Islamophobia among Jewish people. But we invented hummus and falafels together. Couldn't that serve as a foundation (however mushy)?

Returning to the Germans and their Jews: Jewish people in Germany actively support the descendants of perpetrators in their construction of a new identity. I experience this regularly. Sitting in a bar after a reading, eating a Frankfurter hand-cheese* or drinking a beer, the moderator or some other colleague leans forward to discuss a particular text or position of mine. Sometimes I make the mistake of thinking: "Wow, they really want a genuine exchange of ideas." But alas, at the very latest when they start telling me about their SS grandpa, I realize my counterpart has simply switched on their favorite channel of Jew porn. After each and every one of these bar

---

* *Handkäse* is a traditional (regional) German bar snack consisting of hand-pressed, sour milk cheese known for its off-putting scent and often served with oil and vinegar, raw onions, or caraway seeds.

conversations, I feel emptied and hollow. It's like the other side just had all the fun while I could only suppress the urge to cry out: "Next time, just get yourself off alone!"

In these situations, the unequal distribution of power in the relationship between Germans and Jews becomes clear. If I take on their role expectation, I become a Jew for Germans. The Jew for Germans (one could shorten this to JfD)* enjoys telling Germans as much as they can about their experiences with antisemitism, bemoans the fact that such things could still happen in Germany today, and posts depressing videos on Facebook. Their family has a Holocaust story—and even if they don't, they can still assure their audience with credibility that they, too, would have been sent to the camps. Talk of a Judeo-Christian tradition flatters them. They love the German national soccer team. And, of course, they enjoy lighting their menorah at Hanukkah with their friends, the Good Germans, in front of the Brandenburg Gate.

Needless to say, the Theater of Memory also allows for a certain degree of wiggle room: Perhaps one Jew calls for the defense of Israel and another for its destruction. Perhaps a third proposes reconciliation, while a fourth riffles angrily through feuilletons (it will probably not surprise you at this point that the last of these is, in doubt, my favored position).

---

* JfD (*Jude für Deutsche*), an allusion to the far-right political party, AfD (Alternative für Deutschland).

17

A fifth might attend one of those infamous Berlin Meschugge parties* and bring home a German participant awed by their first experience of so much *joie de vivre* and all those beautiful people. But whatever Jewish people do, the most important thing is that they are willing and able afterward—somehow—to confess it to their German peers. I freely admit that I, too, have played along. I've also told Jewish jokes when I had no desire for small talk and wanted to let my counterpart know who here bears the burden of extermination on their shoulders.

Of course, all this has been thought through and described many times before: the implications of inherited victimhood by Alain Finkielkraut, the staging of the Jews in the German Theater of Memory by Michal Bodemann, the increasing identification by Germans with the victim perspective by Ulrike Jureit and Christian Schneider, the self-empowerment of Jewish figures in the books and columns of Maxim Biller. These, and other works, served as starting points for me in my own attempt to comprehend the situation of a new generation of young Jews in Germany.

The second Jewish generation after the Holocaust—my father's generation—described their own efforts for a new start as searching in a vacuum: an emptiness, a glaring

---

* A series of queer-friendly dance parties from the mid-2000s through mid-2010s organized by (then) Berlin-based Israeli DJ Aviv Netter.

absence. To quote Jewish bookseller and publicist Rachel Salamander, it was an attempt "to put down one's roots in nothingness." But some things have changed over the last decades. I belong to the first cohort of Jewish people in Germany to be accompanied by Jewish institutions from preschool, through grade school, and on through my doctoral studies. The great absence described by Rachel Salamander is still palpable, but there is no longer a vacuum: It has been filled by a new Jewish diversity that has also manifested itself in new Jewish institutions. This development was facilitated by the large-scale migration of Jewish people to Germany at the beginning of the 1990s. Which means the overwhelming majority of Jewish people here today are also part of that quarter of the German population with a migration history.

In an increasingly diverse society, Jewish people need not remain committed to their roles in the Theater of Memory, nor Germans to their need to distance themselves from National Socialism. I am convinced that there are ways out of this historical loop. But the alternatives, as James Baldwin demonstrates, begin with the prerequisite that we—as individuals, as well as collectively—ask ourselves in what ways history has written itself into our thought and into our own self-conception: the ways in which we discuss Germany and Judaism, German culture and its diversity, belonging and integration. And in this regard, it seems like we are currently experiencing setbacks. The AfD has returned to models of *völkisch*-ethnonationalist tradition with unmistakable historical affiliations; big party politics follows at their heels. Many may have hoped that German history would not repeat itself, that things could finally return to normal for this country. Instead, the developments of the past years have demonstrated a disturbing proximity to the ideas that precipitated and facilitated National Socialism.

2

NORMALITY RELOADED: SCHLAAAAAND

I FEEL LIKE I HAVE to dedicate some space to the concept of "normality"—that all-too-beloved subject of German conversation. There are few things in the political discourse of this country that carry as positive an affect in their connotation as this word. The Germans want to be *normal*. The Germans want to *finally* be normal *again*. They want to be a *normal* country and a *normal* people again *at long last*. Do those words actually make you feel anything? I'd really like to know. Because then you, too, might come to know this oceanic (nationalistic) feeling that flows between myself and my fellow citizens like a tidal wave—no matter if the topic at hand is as harmless as a soccer match of the German national team.

I grew up in the 1990s and the early 2000s. A time in which everyone tried to convince themselves that German history was all a thing of the past. And I mean, sure: It was a nasty bit of history, but the Germans had learned their lesson now and we were all a part of this new, refined and Reunified Germany. And even if Auschwitz hadn't been a self-help camp for Jews, at least the Germans had learned from their mistakes. From now on, Jewish people should live as equals among equals. Of course, this came with a few hooks and barbs. Hooks:* lol. Because the categorical abolition of antisemitism also meant that the German present was immunized against any question of possible continuities. And this actually is the prevailing law of the land, too: According to the verdict of a judge in Munich's district court responsible for matters of the press, a person could only be described as a "rabid antisemite" if they vocally expressed their antisemitism while at the same time passing no judgment on the Third Reich and its actions (Broder, "So schafft man").

This is actually absurd. Very few contemporary German antisemites would still publicly demand the extermination of the world's Jews. And it is also historically inaccurate to reduce all antisemitism to National Socialism—over its long and storied history, antisemitism rarely meant the complete annihilation of *all* Jewish people. Or even just a measly little pogrom. For the longest time, antisemitism was just a standard part of "normality" in Christian society. To argue that its most extreme expression should stand in for its base definition is like claiming rape is the only form of sexism. Or racism can only mean the literal enslavement of other human beings. The worst-case scenario *cannot* set the

---

*   The German word for swastika is *Hakenkreuz*: hooked cross.

standard for discrimination—though it should serve as an example for just how bad things might become. And here, Henryk M. Broder makes a convincing point (though his other political opinions have become increasingly erratic): "And so, one abolishes antisemitism on a juridical level [. . .] No antisemite is foolish enough to identify their antisemitism with the Nazis. They instead distance themselves from the NS camarilla and proudly proclaim that the Israelis are doing the same thing to the Palestinians that the Nazis did to the Jews." Defining antisemitism solely through the lens of National Socialist-era hatred for the Jews has become a convenient way of resolving the problems of the present day. And, of course, it's not so far removed from the truth of Germany's new self-image, which *is* based (among other things) on the assertion that German antisemitism has long since been successfully overcome.

The claim that Germany has overcome its antisemitism is also shared, particularly, by many of those same people who publicly support *völkisch* and antisemitic positions. And, of course, this observation doesn't solely apply to journalist Jürgen Elsässer—who successfully defended himself in the aforementioned lawsuit against politician Jutta Ditfurth's claim that he is a rabid antisemite. The AfD are not above publicly presenting themselves as the defenders of Germany's Jews (Kamann, "AfD"). But it's too easy always to just point your finger at the Far Right, when this self-image remains true across the spectrum of mainstream media and politics. Our Constitution grounds Germany's political power in the people. And—at the very latest with the 2006 World Cup—those people presented themselves as united in their desire to express a positive national identity. Across the political spectrum and with absolutely no hesitation. Germany was normal again. Germany no longer needed to suppress its national pride.

Now I didn't just grow up during this period of normalization; I also grew up in 1990s Berlin. For my parents (and their circle of friends), there was never a shred of doubt that any product with the German national flag printed on it would never find its way into our shopping carts. And not because someone ever said this explicitly. But because we all wanted it that way. Even as a little kid, I could have already made that call myself. And then came 2006. And with 2006 came all the flags. What surprised me about the whole thing was this rhetoric of celebrating the black-red-and-gold euphoria as some kind of almost unchallenged, collective sense of relief. "A time to make friends!" was the official English slogan; but a more literal translation of the German "*Die Welt zu Gast bei Freunden*" [the world visiting friends] really drives the absurdity home. I can remember conflict after conflict with all those same friends and family who had previously avoided buying any product with the German flag on it—simply because I didn't share their sudden enthusiasm. Then as now, I believe that this newfound identification with the German nation says a lot about those people who found themselves caught up in the festivities. I've said it before, and I'm happy to say it again: I preferred the 1990s, and I didn't shed one single tear for repressed nationalism or national-flag-withdrawal syndrome.

In 2006, people started acting like they'd all just shrugged off a long-carried burden. "We're finally allowed to do this again!" they cried, while painting flags on their faces as though they had forgotten everything they'd ever told me when I was still a child. Their cries already said it all. Because those who say "finally" are experiencing a relief that they may do something again. And those who say "again"—in this case—are referring to a time when the German flag could flutter without any strange feelings of guilt. And when was that again? Right: the Nazi days. And then, there's this "we're allowed"—as though someone had forbidden someone else from doing something. And who was that again? Ah, the good German tradition of seeing foreign intervention behind every home-made problem—foreign agents who manipulate and regulate what the poor German people are allowed to do. But let's face it: At the end of the day, the only thing the German people opposed during the World Cup was their own guilty consciences—as homemade as a cake baked by your favorite Nazi grandma. The Germans experienced the 2006 World Cup as a collective feeling of relief that they were finally allowed to fly their German flags again. Just like before. And I call this perpetrator solidarity.

I'm sorry if it sounds like I'm trying to pin some kind of collective guilt on all the Germans here. No, actually, I'm only a little sorry. Because my friends and I didn't miss that German flag. *Y'all* were the ones who missed it. *Y'all* painted it on *your* cheeks. *Y'all* stood on the beer benches and sang the national anthem. From the jubilant mobs to the clever editorials, *y'all* celebrated that Germany was finally a country you could be proud of again. And suddenly, everyone wanted to tell the world how cool it felt to be German. And that's why I make this distinction in my book when I say "the Germans." I'd like to underscore here that those Germans behaved like they fell right in line with their perpetrator past and not the history of the victims at all. And, speaking strictly biographically, that *is* mostly correct. But it opens up a strange tension between claims of—on the one hand—repressed national feelings and—on the other hand—the assertion that we were all "liberated" on May 8, 1945.

And here, at last, we come to something that is no longer an individual but a structural problem. Because Jewish people in this country don't identify with the German crimes. And as such, they also don't identify with this uniquely German desire for relief. And so, of course, Jewish people can disturb the Germans in their process of normalization—and yet their presence in this society also remains a necessary prerequisite for Germany's new self-image. And this paradoxical mechanism is nothing new.

Over the nearly two thousand years of Christian dominance, Jews have been a central point of reference for Christian self-conception—and with it, sociopolitical convictions, movements, and theories. Sometimes the Jews were the murderers of Jesus, sometimes usurers, and sometimes they possessed only the logic of unskilled animals. Communism was a Jewish conspiracy, but capitalism was also the incarnation of Jewish greed. The literal money quote from Karl Marx: "What is the secular basis of Judaism? Practical need, self-interest. What is the worldly religion of the Jew? Huckstering. Who is his worldly God? Money" (*Zur Judenfrage*, 42). During the First World War, British Foreign Secretary Lord Balfour promised the Jews a Jewish state in Palestine because he feared that international Jewry would otherwise side with the Germans. And then, what irony of history: Germany decided—allegedly in self-defense—first to persecute and then to exterminate *all* Jewish people. Anyone who demanded the return of dispossessed Jewish property after the War was just supporting capitalism. Or at least that's what Jewish Communist Leo Bauer observed, according to his firsthand account of Walter Ulbricht's commentary before the founding of the German Democratic Republic: "We were always opposed to Jewish capitalists every bit as much so as the non-Jewish capitalists. And had Hitler not dispossessed them of their wealth, we would have done so ourselves after seizing power" (Hartewig, 275). And, of course, after 1968 those who continued to support Israel were Jewish imperialists. Again and again, Jewish people find themselves at the center of the self-image of some opposing ideology or political movement. Over and over and over.

The German public—and with it, a great number of my own associates—outed themselves during the 2006 World Cup as people who believed their national feelings had somehow previously been repressed. I couldn't relate to this feeling in the slightest. Quite the opposite: I had always been filled with the deepest respect for those athletes who refused to sing along with the national anthem—something that happened much more frequently before 2006. And back then, it didn't always stir controversy—like we see now with Mesut Özil—when an athlete didn't move their lips along in time. And lest we forget—because people forget these kinds of things so quickly—the lyrics and melody of the German national anthem are the same as those the Nazis sang. I know, I know: It's ancient history. And the tune was composed by Haydn centuries before the Nazis. And the lyrics were written in the nineteenth century by Fallersleben (who, by the way, was a pretty rabid antisemite himself). But still. I think after the twentieth century, we should be able to respect someone's decision not to sing songs of praise to Germany if they don't feel like it. And just leave it at that.

If someone really has the impression that they've surrendered to a forbidden feeling when they wave a flag or sing the national anthem—well, that person has a problem. Just like I don't smoke my cigarettes and then claim that someone forced me to. But it seems like we—as a society—are still painfully far away from such an outlook on personal responsibility for one's actions. It's been a good decade now since that World Cup, and now the AfD has managed to establish itself in the Bundestag as the party of We're-Not-Allowed-To-Say-Anything-Anymore. And let's just reflect on that for a minute: One of their most prominent politicians recently demanded Germany's resurrection at the Kyffhäuser and called for the German Kaiser Barbarossa to awaken and save the nation in its hour of great need.[*] I had to check my calendar. Yep. We're still in the twenty-first century and not 1843—the year Heinrich Heine penned *Deutschland. Ein Wintermärchen* [Germany: A Winter's Tale]. But maybe it's time for a reread. You'd certainly find plenty of parallels.

After the illustrious story I've just recounted, would it really be that hard to draw a connection between the 2006 World Cup and the AfD's ascension to the Bundestag in 2017?

---

[*]   The Kyffhäuser is a mountain in eastern Germany of mythological and historical significance to German nationalism—according to legend, Kaiser Barbarossa is sleeping under the mountain, awaiting the call to rise and reunite Germany. The legend is satirized in Heinrich Heine's politically charged epic *Deutschland. Ein Wintermärchen*.

The former signified the normalization of nationalism and national symbols, the latter demanded that corresponding concepts return front-row-center to the political theater. When a *völkisch*-ethnonationalist agenda seems both intuitive and plausible for 12.6 percent of the German population in the federal elections, I think that's cause for more consideration. Because this, too, is a part of German normality. German addiction to cigarettes. German guiding culture, if you will. And it's possible that conservative politicians meant something else entirely when they called for German guiding culture in the years before the election. But does it really matter what they claim they wanted, when it's so easy to observe what actually transpired?

What transpired is that the legend of Germany becoming good again was put to a pretty serious test. But it doesn't seem like very many people even noticed. Instead, the concept of positive national identity is still making the rounds—entirely uninhibited—across the entire political spectrum: #normalization. A normalization that—surprise, surprise—came hand in hand with the reactivation of nationalism, antisemitism, and chauvinism. It stands to reason then that educational scholar Astrid Messerschmidt refers to Germany as a "post-National Socialist society." And if you still aren't convinced, have a look at the early works of Henryk M. Broder or the unrivaled polemicist Eike Geisel. May he rest in peace.

*

Now, you can probably already tell from my language and my style that I'm a relatively young author. As a representative of a new generation, you might expect me to say something *about* this generation—that I might even have something to say *to* it. Well, then I guess I'd have to reveal myself as a participant observer: collecting my observations from the Baltic beaches of Rügen, house parties in Cologne, family gatherings in Köpenick, and the urinals of Munich's clubs. Time and again, someone brushes their sweaty hair out of their face, clutches their beer a little tighter, and whispers how German history may have been pretty bad, but all that stuff we learned in school was really just too much. "What do you mean *too much*?" I ask. You know: "Too much Holocaust," they say. All that stuff happened a really long time ago. And here my participant observee has already outed themself as a member of the perpetrator collective—even before I can so much as whisper: "Where did your granny get her set of silver spoons?" Bam! Am I being too thin-skinned? Or have you, perhaps, become too thick-skinned yourself?

It seems that young Germans today have lost the fascination with the Holocaust that their parents still maintained. It must have been a charming thing for the first generation to be born after: confronting their Nazi parents with a truly moral transgression. And that worked well enough. It allowed them to stand rhetorically on the other, better side of the debate. Patricide can be fun. But that fun had an expiration

31

date. And it seems to have lost its appeal for the children of the patricidal. This generation only retained the boring certainty that they—along with their parents and grandparents—are part of a diffuse and never truly self-consciously reflected collective of perpetrators. And so it's not surprising that they've lost interest in these perpetrator memories. But, alas, there was an argumentative salvation already at hand: The Germans weren't defeated; they were liberated. Just like the Jews!

I'll come back to this idea shortly.

German psychologist and pedagogue Birgit Rommelspacher describes a given society's prevailing cultural norms as "dominant culture" [*Dominanzkultur*]. Dominant culture does not necessarily represent the perspective of the majority of those living in a country. It represents the sum total of a society's dominant imaginaries and practices. Like, for example, the omnipresent demand for integration, or the inescapable dynamic between Germans and Jews. The demand for normality is also an expression of German dominant culture. And because its affirmation relies on the staging of a German-Jewish reconciliation, I, too, posit "*the Germans*" and "*the Jews*" in contrast to one another. And let me make this clear: This is *not* because I truly believe that there is a clearly delineated *German* or *Jewish* community: In truth there are neither "Germans" nor "Jews," nor anything resembling a community. When I speak, then, of a *German* perspective or a *German* desire, I merely wish to highlight that a particular desire regulates the representation of Jewish people in the Theater of Memory. Dominant culture at its finest.

But what does it mean to play the Jew for the Germans? What does it mean to play a different role in the German Theater of Society—the ultraliberal Muslim or the socially conservative gay? And what are the consequences of developing a German positionality out of this performance? Does it provide satisfaction? Would I like to concede this satisfaction to others? What elements of our history or our present must first be rendered invisible in order to do so? Esteemed readers, when I tell you to de-integrate, this means so much more than Jewish emancipation from the too-narrow expectations of our current role. It's about a very fundamental reflection on the relationship between Germany's dominant culture and the positionalities of its minorities. De-integration means reflecting critically on our roles—the roles that each and every one of us assumes in our daily lives. This is urgent, critical social work, for the demands for integration and the Theater of Memory reach far back into the dirty reservoirs of German history—both before and after 1945.

3

THE EARLY YEARS:
INTEGRATING NAZIS

IF WE WANT TO DISCUSS great accomplishments for integration in the decades after 1945, we'd have to be talking about the integration of former National Socialists. And this goes for both German societies in the years after the War. Let this roll around on your tongue for a minute and savor the bad taste: The early Federal Republic of Germany spent a good deal more effort attending to the fates of convicted Nazi criminals than it did taking care of the many victims of this defunct, criminal regime. We can observe this in the use of a term like "reparations" [*Wiedergutmachung*]. Now, I tend to think about reparations primarily in reference to compensating those various victim groups of National Socialist violence. But in the early years after the War, this concept included not merely the payment of remunerations to former forced laborers, but also the rehabilitation of convicted Nazi criminals who had gone into hiding after the War (Frei, 89). A statistic published by the US government shows that only a minority of the West German population rejected National Socialism as "a bad thing" in the initial two years after the defeat of Nazi Germany (Friedrich, 41). A moderate Nazi leader (whatever that's supposed to mean) could, in all likelihood, have won a democratic majority in 1945 or 1946. Which would, of course, support my theory that the majority of Germans were not liberated at all, but defeated. Vanquished. Conquered. They lost the War. And they begrudgingly accepted their new democratic reality like the diagnosis of a chronic illness.

If one were so inclined, one could read any number of works on this subject. Books like Ralph Giordano's 1987 *Die zweite Schuld* [The Second Guilt], or Norbert Frei's comprehensive 1996 study *Vergangenheitspolitik* [The Politics of the Past], which traces the founding of the Federal Republic. Dominik Rigoll's 2013 *Staatsschutz in Westdeutschland: Von der Entnazifizierung zur Extremistenabwehr* [State Security in West Germany: From Denazification to Resisting Extremists] would round out this survey of modern historiography nicely. Norbert Frei sums up his findings on the political situation in Germany during the decade after the War as follows:

The self-evidence and blatant manner at the beginning of the 1950s with which both politics and the general public intervened on behalf of war criminals and Nazi perpetrators convicted by the Allied Powers—demanding both their release as well as their social reintegration—are, indeed,

> perhaps the most surprising and utterly disturbing finding
> of my research. (16)

The ongoing support of National Socialists from the majority of the German population demonstrates, for Frei, the high level of social cohesion that their ideology continued to maintain. And where there is ideology, there is also an argument. A counterargument that developed swiftly in opposition to the Allies' program of denazification was that small-fry German followers were being condemned as Nazi sharks. They had only been following orders after all, and were now being treated like the most serious war criminals. But this claim of a supposedly external allocation of "collective guilt" is merely a classic trope of denial. One that continues to rear its ugly head right up to the present day. The US military regime that ruled in Germany after the War never made such an accusation. They actually went to considerable lengths in their legislation to distinguish between different levels of culpability. As early as March 1946, they introduced the categories of "major offenders" [*Hauptschuldige*], "offenders" [*Belastete*], as well as "activists" [*Aktivisten*], "lesser offenders" [*Minderbelastete*], "followers" [*Mitläufer*], and "exonerated persons" [*Entlastete*] in their Law for the Liberation from National Socialism and Militarism [*Gesetz zur Befreiung von Nationalsozialismus und Militarismus*].

With the introduction of this law, the US military government passed their responsibility for the political conviction of Nazi criminals on to their German counterparts. And given the aforementioned political atmosphere among the general population, it is not at all surprising that political implementation of these laws remained rather limited on the part of the Germans. We see this in the low number of convictions from German courts and in the 1949 "Immunity Act" [*Straffreiheitsgesetz*], which provided amnesty to those who were convicted with less than a half-year's imprisonment or a year's probation. And so, instead of the differentiated convictions envisioned by the Law for the Liberation from National Socialism and Militarism, the very opposite ensued. Under pressure from a large portion of the German populace, the rehabilitation of already-convicted Nazi criminals followed—including many of those "major offenders." What a triumphant start for a country that today claims to have overcome its National Socialist past in exemplary fashion.

When I run this tragedy before my eyes in its full magnitude, I get a tremendous urge to follow painter Max Liebermann's example and eat as much as possible just to throw it all up again. I'll return to my gag reflex in the chapter on artistic reprocessing. For the time being, I'm going to exercise patience and accept that it could very well have been nigh impossible to establish the Federal Republic of Germany—or, in similar fashion, the German Democratic Republic—without the rehabilitation of some Nazi goons. This is a question of sheer numbers: Conservative estimates point to between

200,000 and 300,000 people who were directly responsible for the mass murder of Europe's Jewish population alone. The total number of supporters, white-collar criminals, paper pushers, and confidants would then have been a great deal higher. It could well have been, however, that the majority of the German population at that time was not concerned with differentiating between levels of responsibility at all. That they understood themselves as an ethnic community [*Volksgemeinschaft*] in which one's responsibility as a German was to protect all other Germans.

In his phenomenal work *On the Natural History of Destruction* [*Luftkrieg und Literatur*], originally published in 1997, author W. G. Sebald—who passed on far before his time—investigates the psychological tenacity that made possible the German population's rapid reconstruction of their devastated country and its economy. Sebald concludes that this achievement was based on "the well-kept secret of the corpses built into the foundations of our state, a secret that bound all Germans together in the postwar years, and indeed still binds them, more closely than any positive goal such as the realization of democracy ever could" (13). This passage shakes the very essence of postwar German history as it was taught to me at school and in university: that both West and East Germany were newly founded in opposition to National Socialism and grounded on insight concerning the moral and political mistakes of history. When we consider the veritable wave of Nazi rehabilitation that occurred in West Germany in the early 1950s, we arrive at a far less optimistic interpretation. I'll speak to the specificities of East Germany in just a moment. But in any case, it's very difficult to reconcile these early decades after the defeat of National Socialism with the current self-image of the Good Germans.

As we begin to reassess the narrative of Germany's restart after World War II, other points of coherence become dubious, as well. What, for example, truly underlies the public taboo against antisemitism and National Socialism? Was this really born of new moral insight on the part of the German populace? Or was it not, instead, a product of necessity—entrenching those self-same, old political forces that had reestablished themselves in Germany while presenting a clean slate to the occupying Allied forces? Norbert Frei certainly arrives at a similar argument when he describes the linguistic and conceptual boundaries drawn around antisemitism from the early 1950s on as "attempts at normativizing demarcations, which became increasingly important the more amnesty and integration advanced, threatening to debase the anti-National Socialist founding consensus of West Germany from 1945" (23). That's a bitter pill in and of itself. But it leaves a substantially worse taste in your mouth if you consider how the ongoing rehabilitation and integration of former Nazi officials coincided with the public exclusion of former resistance fighters. From the mid-1950s on, these people increasingly came to be considered "politically untrustworthy"—after all, they had already revealed themselves as willing to resist the structures of the German state before. In his 2013 *Staatsschutz in Westdeutschland*, historian Dominik Rigoll traces this process of marginalization up to the 1970s. And if we can acknowledge that a continuity with National Socialist thought extended far beyond the 1950s, this would probe a very neuralgic spot when it comes to Germany's self-assurance: the catharsis. When did this catharsis actually take place?

Perhaps my line of reasoning here might raise a few objections. Perhaps some of you would like to intercede and note that we're still talking about the history of a relatively young republic—a country slowly emerging from the shadows of National Socialism. 1968 and all of that. But I would want to counter your observation with an objection of my own: Yes, this is the story we all learned, but it's simply not accurate enough. Because in the Federal Republic of Germany, it was precisely the policy of integrating former Nazis that inhibited a critique of ongoing continuities with National Socialism and a public condemnation of its crimes. And so, rather than a self-critical reflection on the continuities of things like anti-semitism or anti-Slavism, the first decades passed in relative silence. And this also influenced those who came of age in the last years of the Nazi regime.

The continuity of Nazi children with their parents' generation is a core thesis of Götz Aly's polemical study *Unser Kampf*

1968—ein irritierter Blick zurück [Our Struggle, 1968: A Look Back in Irritation]. In this 2008 monograph, Aly contradicts the widespread perception that Germany's reprocessing and reengagement with its Nazi history was implemented by the 1968 generation, or at least, that they were largely responsible for initiating this conversation. Aly poses, instead, that individual attempts to reengage with this history had already begun in the early 1960s—attempts that were largely dismissed or ignored by the so-called 68ers. One need only consider the demarcations that emerged around this time: the evil Nazi parents on one side, and the good, leftist students on the other. A new generation that broke the silence by accusing their own parents. And of course, this much *is* true. But these accusations also permitted a new generation to distance themselves from questions concerning their own continuity with National Socialist mentalities and biases. Götz Aly concludes that it would have been unthinkable for the 68ers to reflect on ideological or political continuities with their National Socialist parents because their very self-conception did not permit it.

Even decades later, the extent to which Jewish people in Germany felt ostracized by their own leftist comrades becomes glaringly apparent when you read the essays and autobiographies of the Jewish protagonists of the 1968 generation—for example, Micha Brumlik, Dan Diner, Wolfgang Seibert, or Henryk M. Broder. Even Maxim Biller—born too late to have participated in the '68 movement directly—still derides the movement as the rebellion of Nazi children against their Nazi parents. Broder later wrote an essay in the early 1980s that provides an account of the so-called "red decade." He titled his work: "Ihr bleibt die Kinder eurer Eltern" [You Remain Your Parents' Children]. In this essay, articulated as a farewell note to his former leftist comrades-in-arms, Broder accuses them of willful ignorance vis-à-vis their own affinity to the mentalities of National Socialism—antisemitism in particular. Broder writes:

> What I am accusing you of is a refusal to recognize the connection between cause and effect when it came to yourselves. Of behaving as though you were a new people: removed from the stench of the kitchen from which you all emerged—as though you all were born, instead, into a vacuum that filled only after your own arrival. But you absorbed more in your cradles than the sound of your own rattles. You were fed not merely porridge, but also the biases and predilections of your mothers and fathers. Their ways of thinking and of feeling. This is a thought that has escaped all of you, even today.

Perhaps it was this very refusal of the 68ers to reflect on the critique of National Socialism's misanthropy when it came to themselves that ultimately led to Vergangenheits*bewältigung* [overcoming the *past*] becoming the central concept for processing Germany's Nazi inheritance. The demarcation of boundaries between the past and their own present that this term implies became a central building block in the construct of the second generation's new German self-image. And it remained this way for the generations that followed. Even today. There could not be such a thing as Gegenwarts*bewältigung* [overcoming the *present*] if the price was one's own goodness. The result is a far-reaching absence of historical (self-)comprehension when it comes to the post-National Socialist German present day.

And this false perception reveals itself time and again in the ongoing influence of the anti-leftist, antidemocratic reflexes that were written into the very structures of the German government—things like its intelligence service (and their personnel)—from the inception on. I need only provide a few examples here: Following the demonstrations at the 2017 G20 summit in Hamburg, leftist projects were raided across Germany. Those who participated in the demonstrations faced draconian punishments, along with an intensification in the overall scale of potential ramifications for their crimes. On the other hand, the terrorist attacks of the National Socialist Underground (NSU)—which resulted in ten deaths—were not even officially recognized as neo-Nazi activity for *ten years*, and have since resulted in only one single change in criminal prosecution procedures. And this, on a state—not federal—level. The political party Die Linke [The Left] is officially under observation from the German intelligence service. The far-right AfD, on the other hand—despite its concrete ties to identitarian, *Reichsbürger*,[*] and neo-Nazi movements—remained blissfully free of any official declarations of suspicion up to the time of the original German composition of this work. And despite increasing attention from the intelligence community, it was not until March 2022—during the translation of the book you currently hold in your hands—that they were finally deemed worthy of official observation. Meanwhile, almost daily arson attacks on refugee asylum homes have been occurring now in Germany for years. But I haven't heard anything about government raids to counteract these crimes. And, even despite mountains of contrary evidence, this has not prevented spokespeople for the New Right like Martin Lichtmesz and Caroline Sommerfeld from bemoaning the "clemency of the German state when it comes to antifascist violence" (26).

Sorry. Excuse me while I suppress my urge to vomit once again.

But without sufficient knowledge of Germany's postwar history, I would be unable to make sense of this simultaneous

---

[*] The *Reich* Citizens' Movement is an amorphous collection of rightwing groups whose ideology centers around the illegitimacy of the modern German state and allegiance to various pre-1945 incarnations of the German Reich (including the belief that a 'legitimate' German imperial government still exists somewhere in exile and increasing identification with followers of the US far-right QAnon conspiracy).

acceptance of rightwing violence and persecution of leftwing crimes, the incessant demands for German guiding culture against the alleged dominance of a leftwing, liberal mainstream. Because none of it corresponds with my own perception of things. It is only when viewed through the lens of German history that it becomes clear how the contradictions of the present day derive from National Socialism and its continuities in postwar Germany.

And with this historical perspective in mind, I arrive at a completely different conclusion than Per Leo, Max Steinbeis, and Daniel-Pascal Zorn in their 2017 *Mit Rechten reden* [Talking with the Right]. The so-called "New" Right does not in any way draw its strength from the alleged (or real) lack of a theoretical basis on the part of the "New Left"—whoever that's supposed to be. Instead, both political positions align against the question of post-1945 German identity. Because all of them belong to those who were born after—they are leftists and born after, feminists and born after, liberals and born after, alongside the rightwingers, ethnonationalists, and antisemites who were born after, too. Being "born after" ties together the whole range of Germany's political spectrum: It makes accomplices of them all, while it imposes a shared desire to dissociate from National Socialism onto Jewish people and other minoritized groups in this country. I will come back to this observation, but at this point, I feel the need to underscore that Germany's dominant culture—regardless of political perspective—intersects with this problem.

One figure looms large over the change of political perspective and the gradual development of Germany's self-rehabilitation—someone who often wrongfully goes unrecognized: Martin Walser. Do you all remember the speech this author gave back in 1998 at St. Paul's Church in Frankfurt am Main? He was receiving the Peace Prize of the German Book Trade [*Friedenspreis des Deutschen Buchhandels*] at the time, and used the opportunity to really cut loose. Perhaps the topic had already begun to churn around inside him while he was a still-leftist observer at the Frankfurt Auschwitz trials in 1964. Who knows? In case you can't remember precisely what it was that he said in his speech, that's not a problem. I couldn't either. I was probably watching *Sandmann*[*] at the time. Or maybe my mother covered my ears and eyes in horror. At least I hope she did. But it's so easy these days to read or listen to it all again online. And I'm old enough to deal with this kind of bullshit now. If you can tolerate a gory splatter film, you can listen to Martin Walser, too. A short excerpt from his speech, if you please:

No serious person denies Auschwitz; no sane person quibbles over the horrors of Auschwitz. And yet, when the media

---

[*]   A beloved German stop-motion children's bedtime show.

dangles this history before me every day, I notice that something in me rises up against this constant presentation of our shame. Rather than feel grateful for this incessant presentation, I start to look away.

Yeah, I know, that's all a bit ambiguous. It could probably go either way, right? But it continues on a very definite trajectory:

But what suspicion we fall under when we say that Germans are a completely ordinary people! A completely normal society? In the discussions around the Holocaust Memorial in Berlin, posterity will be able to observe what happened to those who took responsibility for the consciences of others: Concrete poured across the center of the capital as a football field-sized nightmare. The monumentalization of shame.

Oops. Did I just quote an excerpt from a speech by Björn Höcke by mistake—that far-right winger for the AfD? In case you're taking notes: Höcke *did* also describe the Holocaust Memorial in 2015 as a "monument of shame." But Martin Walser called it the "monumentalization of shame" seventeen years earlier. My bad. The quotation above really does belong to Walser. Perhaps we can all try to remember this together. And perhaps it would also be worthwhile to note: "monumentalization" equaled a Peace Prize for Walser, but "monument" resulted in proceedings for Höcke's expulsion from the party. Expulsion from the far-right AfD. Walla.

At the time, Walser's speech would probably have been more or less waved through without much uproar if the then president of the Central Council of Jews in Germany, Ignatz Bubis, and his wife, Ida Bubis, hadn't decided to remain seated while the rest of the audience rose to give Walser a standing ovation at the conclusion of his speech (I've got to give an additional nod of respect here to theologian and former East German civil rights activist Friedrich Schorlemmer, who remained seated, as well). Over the coming months, a protracted exchange eventually arose between an enraged Bubis and a stubborn Walser, who remained unable to comprehend how Bubis could describe his speech as an act of "intellectual arson." A Jew had refused to smile and nod at this new Reunified-German nationalism—and those who would attempt to do such a thing to a Good German . . . well, this insubordination demanded punishment. And Walser made Bubis aware of this when he—for whatever reason—eventually attempted to extend Walser the hand of reconciliation. Walser ignored his outstretched arm. Which, to be perfectly honest, was a pretty extraordinary move for a German author of his generation.

But now, let us leave West Germany for a moment. How were things in the German Democratic Republic? The starting point was different for East Germany, since the new political

leadership consisted explicitly of those who had been persecuted by the old. There was no need to overcome personal
entanglements with National Socialism. The problem here
was also the German populace itself, which had—prior to
1945—in no way behaved as it should have according to
Communist theories of fascism. While exiled in Moscow
or Mexico, an expectation had developed that the German
people would—at the latest after the defeat at Stalingrad—
rise up against the Nazi government. But they didn't. Quite
the contrary. National Socialist ideology continued to hold
sway even as the Nazi bigwigs gathered in a Berlin bunker
to poison their own children and then commit mass suicide.
Just like in the West, the majority of Germans living in the
Soviet occupation zone remained Nazis to the bitter end.
A reality that did not mesh well with the new, prevailing
Communist ideology.

How does one proceed as the Communist government of a
Nazi population? First off, the Soviet Union made unmistak-
ably clear who had the final say. At the very latest, after Soviet
tanks crushed the attempted uprising on June 17, 1953, there
remained no illusion as to who the true rulers of East Germany
really were. But because it is tedious to maintain a political
system in the long term through tanks alone, Communist
leadership sought out new forms of political legitimation.
And they located these in claims of a common, shared antifascism that met the population halfway in their own desire for

political and moral amnesty. And so, after the high officials of National Socialism's apparatus of power were removed under great fanfare, the average members of the National Socialist German Workers' Party (NSDAP) were largely integrated into the new Socialist Unity Party of Germany (SED) unquestioned—as citizens without prior party affiliation. And along with this transition came an antifascist self-image from the Communist leadership. Not exactly an unattractive offer of self-identification for the first decades.

I'm going to make an exception here and not make light of the situation. Because Communists really were the most persecuted political group under National Socialism. To such an extent that they *could* legitimately claim to have founded the German Democratic Republic as a counter-state to Nazi Germany. And this claim also convinced many Communist Jewish people to return to Germany. But here, too, of course, they were allocated a particular function. Bodemann describes this as follows: "Similar to West Germany, the presence of Jews served as living proof of the dogma that Nazism had been eradicated 'to its very roots' in the German Democratic Republic" (*Gedächtnistheater*, 107). Such confirmation of the antifascist state through its Jews acquired increasing relevance, the more unstable the connection grew between the political leadership and the general population. Adding to a growing international interest in Jewish themes, the vanishing legitimacy of the East German state could serve as another possible justification for its sudden interest in Jewish life from the 1980s on—after decades of almost complete ignorance. And it is, perhaps, not irrelevant that the German Democratic Republic collapsed just as the Nazi generation itself began its own decline. The majority of the East German population, it seems, had only needed Communist antifascism so long as it detached them from National Socialism and continued to sweep antisemitic encroachments under the rug of political self-conception. By 1989, the socialist state had finally fulfilled these obligations. And as a consequence, the antifascist narrative was replaced by the new-old German nationalism—something refugees in the 1990s experienced with brutal clarity. Hoyerswerda and Rostock were only the beginning.[*]

And now, after some brief reflections on these two lands before time, I'd like to return to the contemporary claim that both postwar Germanies shed their National Socialism in the ensuing decades like old skin. On the basis of my short reviews of both East and West German postwar history, this interpretation strikes me as less of a historical reconstruction than a simple projection of Germany's contemporary self-image onto its past. At the same time, it is precisely the claim of catharsis that makes the return of nationalist and *völkisch*

---

[*] The sites of xenophobic riots in the early 1990s that resulted in widespread violence and arson attacks against residences in predominantly (im)migrant neighborhoods.

discourses possible again today in the political mainstream in the first place. From the Reunification of 1989 to Martin Walser in 1998, from the 2006 World Cup to the ascension of the AfD to the Bundestag in 2017: It's always the same pattern. Autonomous political positions—such as being skeptical of the national anthem, national flag, or national identity—become externalized through innumerable interjections and symbolic gestures. Reticence or self-criticism—when it comes to national issues—are then perceived as having been imposed by dubious "outside forces": a foreign power, an elitist leftwing discourse, or the alleged ruling political class. Those who remain seated today when all others clap, or those who remain skeptical when public spaces dissolve into black-red-and-gold ecstasy, are branded as traitors and unpatriotic knaves. They are no longer worthy of reconciliation.

And yet, I would maintain that my friends and I are part of this country, too—even if we don't identify with this new German national pride. Even when the return of German flags sparks no joy for us. The community of German perpetrators and their descendants have to accept that a part of this country's population doesn't share in their desire for so-called normalization. During my childhood in 1990s Berlin, concepts like *Heimat* and *Leitkultur* were parked in the junkyards of political ideology. They may be back out on the road now with provisional license plates, but their emissions still don't meet environmental standards. And I view their return as a shock and an affront to my way of life. And that of my friends. We are not part of some so-called Judeo-Christian tradition. We never have been. But we are a part of this country that exists beyond the babble of homeland, guiding culture, and integration. And that means we won't accept the roles ascribed to us for the staging of German normality.

There was a time when Jewish people here wanted to play along. But that train has left the station. And back then, Germans were driving the locomotive.

4

THE THEATER OF INTEGRATION! *LEITKULTUR* AND MINISTRIES OF *HEIMAT*

FOR THE PAST TWO DECADES, the word "integration" has been used in Germany to describe its approach to diversity. Not a single democratic party platform neglects to center this term in discussions of social belonging. No discussion panels about migration are complete without someone underscoring the importance of integration. But what does this term really mean anyway? The Federal Office for Migration and Refugees (BAMF) should probably know. Their website defines integration as a "long term process" with the goal that "all people living permanently and legally in Germany be included in its society." BAMF's English website states that integrating immigrants "ensures that everyone who lives legally in Germany is able to exercise their numerous freedoms and make the best use of their skills and abilities." But this also includes the mandate that immigrants "observe our rules and regulations and respect our values" as well as stressing the importance of "learning the German language and providing for your own livelihood." I believe we call that fostering and forcing. So, language learning and law abidance define the parameters of belonging. OK. But that leaves a few questions unanswered. Who, for example, may transcend their so-called "migration history" and when? How long and how far-reaching does the demand for integration extend? And at what point are you no longer considered an immigrant who refuses to integrate [*Integrationsverweigerer*], but simply a frustrated German?

The concept of integration brushes up against the boundaries between *us* and *them*, between *autochthon* and *foreigner*: between those who were already here and new arrivals. And so, the demand for integration formulates an implicit or explicit assumption of *who* should integrate and *how*. This derives from the fantasy that there is some essential difference between German and non-German ancestry, German and non-German behavior, German and non-German culture. An immediate consequence of this differentiation is that people whose parents come from Israel, Turkey, or Senegal for example—along with people who identify as Muslims or Jews—are treated differently from people whose parents were born in Germany and whose value systems align with those of the German dominant culture. Even when those parents have a German passport and speak German. We can witness the consequences of this differentiation firsthand in the way this society deals with neo-Nazis. They may receive similar accusations (immigrants are also accused of things like a propensity for violent behavior and sociocultural frustration), but I've never heard of anyone questioning or denying their fundamental belonging in Germany. And so, as many migration scholars very rightly point out, the reality of integration, as practiced in this country, is not truly all-encompassing. It is, instead, directed at particular people who come to be classified by various labels: Eastern European Jews, asylum seekers, Turks, migrants, Muslims, economic migrants, refugees, North Africans . . . *and so on and so forth.*

But integration is not merely a demand. It is also a means by which society is conceptualized as a place with an intrinsic center. And so, the different political parties may distinguish themselves in terms of their different biases and trajectories, but they are connected by a shared application of the concept of integration. This commonality is the reason it makes sense to talk about an *integration paradigm.* Similar to the Theater of Memory in which Jewish people are ascribed a role in Germany's self-presentation, the integration paradigm functions only by means of constant, public repetition. And so the fear of social and cultural fragmentation and the salvation of German culture are continuously staged in a kind of Theater of Integration. Its staging requires at least two supporting actors: on the one hand, the exemplary, well-integrated migrant—crowned with something akin to the Integration

Prize of the District of Charlottenburg-Wilmersdorf.* On the other side, lurk the "barbaric, Muslim, rapist hordes of men"† or other similar bogeymen figures who threaten the alleged cultural values of Germany (*Berliner Zeitung*, "Hass-Inhalte").

Anyone who has ever spent any time doing quantitative social research knows that within any group—given a sufficient number of participants—it is possible to find just about anything: athletes and philosophers; violent rapists and meek, passive conformists. And the same truth holds for Germany. Also, for its Jewish and Muslim populations. If you look closely enough, you can identify problems (and solutions) anywhere. But this kind of careful differentiation is not what the Theaters of Memory and Integration are about. Because staging these huge clefts of difference between "us" and "them" serves to stabilize dominant culture. "We treat our women well, the Others don't. We care about our children; the Others traumatize them with ritual circumcision. We eat

---

*   Although the Berlin district of Charlottenburg is frequently ridiculed as a bastion of neoliberal, bourgeois values, this is, in fact, an actual prize: *Integrationspreis des Bezirks Charlottenburg-Wilmersdorf*.

†   Following media reports of mass sexual assaults on the night between New Year's Eve 2015 and New Year's Day 2016, the image of sexually deviant masses of unhinged Muslim men assaulting white German women became a common trope of rightwing talking heads. The above quote is from a 2018 tweet from Beatrix von Storch that resulted in a temporary Twitter ban for the then deputy leader of the far-right AfD.

our pork peacefully; the Others slaughter animals." You get my point. Germany's national image has always been constructed through cultural differentiation. And so it's no coincidence that the culturalization of the Theater of Integration has been condensed into one special German word: *Leitkultur*—guiding culture.

The concept of guiding culture was developed by German political scientist Bassam Tibi in 1996. Originally, it was conceptualized as a shared consensus of European values. But when supplemented with the adjective *German*, "German guiding culture" quickly developed into the favorite battle cry of conservative politicians, who always seemed to locate new applications for this concept in every new integration debate. After a few volatile years, things seemed to have settled down. Up until May 2017, I had actually begun to hope that I'd survived the worst. But then the former Minister of the Interior, Thomas de Maizière, gave an interview with the *Bild am Sonntag* in which he presented the public with ten theses on migration, flight, and the German population: "Thesen zur Leitkultur" [Theses on Guiding Culture]. The conservative de Maizière employs the concept of guiding culture in a targeted manner to underscore how German citizens "maintain [...] in addition to our language, constitution, and respect for fundamental rights [...] something in our innermost being that binds us and distinguishes us from others." And that's the ABC of the integration paradigm.

Then, at the beginning of 2018, Alexander Dobrindt (at that time the chairman of the Bavarian CSU's *Landesgruppe* representatives in the Bundestag) demanded a "conservative revolution" against an alleged "leftist hegemony" in the exploratory talks for forming a new governing coalition with the SPD. The goals of Dobrindt's bizarre proclamation of revolution were nearly identical to those of de Maizière's theses from the year before. According to Dobrindt: "Crosses hang in our classrooms, men and women shake hands, girls participate in physical education, and we show our faces in public." There is no plural form of *Leitkultur*. Guiding culture only works in the singular. And for both Dobrindt and de Maizière, that form is *German*: a monolithic singularity that demands the existence of something like a homogeneous culture—something worthy of being defended at all costs. OK, let's play along for a minute. I'd like to figure out just what the following pillars of "German" culture have in common: the antisemitic pathos trumpet Richard Wagner with Heinrich Heine, the Nazi philosopher Martin Heidegger with Walter Benjamin, the SPD's rightwing striker Thilo Sarrazin with Gorki Theater director Shermin Langhoff? Speaking German? Sharing the basic impulses to eat, breathe, and sleep? To pool these attributes together as an expression of "guiding culture" seems about as precise to me as determining familial relations because we share about half the human genome with that of a banana. Both would only make sense if we didn't even try to align them with empirical, scientific assessments, but recognized them, instead, as the attempt to distance oneself from something else entirely. Something like Muslims or, I don't know, papayas? I never really liked papayas anyway.

But where exactly does it take us when we try to cobble together a concept of guiding culture? Well, Dobrindt's polemical demands in 2018 didn't just call for a "conservative revolution" coincidentally—this served rather to provide a fittingly aggressive backdrop to the discourse at large. He didn't waste a word on the origin of the concept he was employing. And this, too, was not an oversight. Because the blanket claim of German guiding culture can only function if an individual does not base their argument on historic facts. Let's take the concept of conservative revolution for example: This formulation has appeared in a great variety of contexts over the past 150 years. Its most popular application can be traced back to *Die konservative Revolution in Deutschland 1918–1932. Ein Handbuch* [The Conservative Revolution in Germany 1918–1932: A Handbook], a work by the rightwing intellectual Armin Mohler, published in West Germany in 1950. Mohler employs the concept to outline an alliance of authors, intellectuals, and scholars from the Weimar Republic who promoted antiliberal, antidemocratic, and antiegalitarian ideologies. There were some real charmers among them, covering a range stretching from Oswald Spengler to Carl Schmitt and Ernst Jünger. But what remains indisputable is that these same intellectual heroes provided the philosophical and ideological foundations for National Socialism. One could argue that this conservative revolution was a kind of intellectual pregame for 1933.

As early as 1925, Ernst Jünger had penned his own inspirational quote regarding Jewish integration (Mohler later served as Jünger's private secretary in the first years after the War): "In the same measure, however, that the German will increases in its precision and form, the kind of mild delusion that the Jew could ever be German in Germany grows unimaginable. He arrives, instead, at his final option: To be a Jew in Germany, or not to be at all" ("Unsere Politiker"). And the crowd at Madison Square Garden goes wild!* Quite a distinct position when it comes to the topic of integration. And here we also see that Dobrindt is not really a conservative revolutionary at all. For a truly *völkisch* racist would deny those they minoritize any possibility of integration, rather than declare it a prerequisite for participation. And an *Antisemitismusbeauftragter*† would have been unthinkable in the Ministry of *Heimat* back

---

* *Applaus im Sportpalast!* Here the author makes a not-so-veiled reference to Göbbel's 1943 "Total War" speech held at a popular World War II-era indoor sporting arena. A parallel could be drawn with the 1939 German-American Bund rally held at Madison Square Garden, in which 22,000 American fascists gathered in support of both the German Nazi Party and homegrown American fascism.

† Since 2018, the German federal government appoints an Antisemitism Commissioner (in some German state governments, this position is further defined as "Commissioner for Jewish Life and Against Antisemitism").

then (Bauer, "Felix Klein")! But still, this didn't stop Dobrindt from employing such a heavily connoted concept without any attempt at historical contextualization—while demanding in the same article that we defend our "Judeo-Christian tradition." And here our CSU politician reveals a certain sloppiness that he shares with other representatives of German dominant culture: the ability to talk trash while remaining convinced that he's just expressing what everyone else is already thinking anyway.

By the way, I didn't have to search far and wide for that aforementioned quote by Ernst Jünger. I found it on the German Wikipedia page for "*konservative Revolution*." A simple Google search could have saved Dobrindt from the absurdity of his own demand if he had really wanted to avoid a rightwing-populist interpretation of his words. But he didn't want to: #dogwhistle. I didn't think I'd ever write something like this, but: My dearest Ernst Jünger, please rise up from your grave and slap some sense into Dobrindt: *I'll show you what "conservative revolution" means.*

Dobrindt's "ignorance" when it comes to the history of certain political catchphrases is representative of a larger trend among predominantly conservative politicians in Germany who attempt to meld the concept of guiding culture with supposed historical evidence and community symbols. The following are a few more examples of the ways in which guiding culturalists like Dobrindt, de Maizière, or the then newly minted Minister of *Heimat* Horst Seehofer have attempted to bend the present day to the right. After all, Dobrindt claims that crosses hang from the walls of classrooms throughout all of Germany. That certainly is not true in Berlin. In Berlin, we also don't shake every stranger's hand we see on the street because that's gross: I don't know where those hands have been. Maybe Dobrindt does. However, if I know someone well, I give them a hug or a kiss. What does your guiding culture think about that? And in my publicly funded Jewish school (just like in many schools across all of Germany), boys and girls had separate physical education classes from about the age of twelve. So does that mean that innumerable Berliners—along with atheists and public-school kids—aren't a part of Germany's "guiding culture"? And good heavens, what would that mean for the Jewish school in Berlin?

In an interview on March 16, 2018, the freshly elected Minister of *Heimat*, Horst Seehofer, declared that Islam did not belong to Germany. And, unlike in previous years, Chancellor Angela Merkel contradicted Seehofer vehemently: pointing to the four million Muslims living in this country today. To which the former Minister of the Interior, Hans-Peter Friedrich, then chimed in: "It's good that an important member of our government is saying those things that the overwhelming majority of the people [*Volk*] understand as self-evident" (Solms-Laubach, "Seehofer"). Ah, yes. He did say: The majority of the German *Volk*. Is it just me, or does that leave a strange, brown aftertaste in your mouth, too?* Or is this just another one of those German-flag things, where some people feel one way about it and other people see it differently? In any case, a good part of Germany's government seems set on a course to drift ever further to the *völkisch* right on an almost daily basis. Reaching limbo-level lows. And Dobrindt wasn't selling himself short in his polemic when he declared the last fifty years of German politics to have been governed by the evil policy leadership of the 68ers. Those last fifty years included sixteen bitter, crispy-bacon years of Helmut Kohl's leadership. Eight years of Gerhard Schröder's SPD-neoliberalism. Sixteen years of Angela Merkel. Dobrindt's argument then takes a real Dadaist turn for the absurd at its conclusion, when he employs the solidly bourgeois, upper-middle-class Berlin neighborhood of Prenzlauer Berg as a codeword for the alleged dominance of leftist thought in Germany. Hahaha. Hahahaha. Hahahahahahahaha. You can only miss the mark by that much when you're aiming at the capital from the farthest reaches of Bavaria.

But seriously, what's up with this whole "Islam-no-crucifix-yes" bullshit? Why are obnoxious church bells OK on Sundays, but obnoxious muezzins taboo? Who seriously wants to choose German *Schlager* music over hip-hop nowadays? But anyway,

---

* As aforementioned, in Germany the color brown is associated with the Nazi party.

this isn't about deconstructing individual facets when it comes to the idea of German guiding culture. What I want to highlight here is that the cultural nationalism of people like de Maizière or Dobrindt, Seehofer or Friedrich, is the expression of the desires of a *particular* subset of German society. And this subset is claiming the right to determine who belongs here and who doesn't. I would like to resist the claim that any one particular interpretation of German history and Christian culture can count as the norm for present-day Germany. Instead, the idea of a German guiding culture must be rejected for what it is: the battle cry of conservative, rightwing politicians. And these people don't represent all of Germany. They cannot speak for German society as a whole.

With this, I have finally reached a point where I can quote a bit of Kurt Tucholsky. In the final chapter of his 1929 *Deutschland, Deutschland über alles. Ein Bilderbuch* [Germany, Germany Over Everything: A Picture Book] he writes:

> One must think of us when one thinks of Germany: we Communists, young socialists, pacifists, all those of us who love freedom. One has to include us when one thinks of "Germany" [. . .] It's too easy to pretend like Germany consists only of nationalist organizations. Germany is a divided country. And we are part of it. (231)

There is a current rightward shift in German politics that is also expressed in the frequency with which *völkisch* categories are being readopted. It is challenging at times to resist the imposition of its outlook on society. But politics doesn't mean a simple confrontation of one people against another, one culture against the next. Politics is the art of organizing social diversity. Such a concept of society as a place of radical diversity is difficult to reconcile with the fantasy of a German guiding culture derived from the myth of Judeo-Christian tradition (Czollek et al., "Radical Diversity"). The propagation of this fantasy has a two-part effect: The exclusion of Muslims from the realm of German history permits their status in Germany and German culture to be questioned. And the inclusion of Jewish people in this history cements one's own sense of moral authority. Jewish people have a choice in how they react to this attempted annexation. Those who are tickled by this flattery or those who share in the fear of Islam may not agree with my critique. For everyone else, I say to you: De-integrate from the Theater of Memory!

Dobrindt or Seehofer can hang a cross up in their offices if they want to. They can eat weisswurst with sweet mustard for lunch and drink at least one liter of beer a day. I have no problem with that and neither do my friends. And that's precisely the point that fundamentally separates those of us who would defend a concept of radical diversity from those proponents of German guiding culture: We want to create a space in which one can be different without fear, while the other side wants to implement cultural criteria for belonging that by necessity exclude those who don't align with their concept. Cue Dobrindt: "Whoever wants to be in Germany has to live with us—not near or contrary to us. And if you don't agree, then you can leave" ("Wir brauchen"). The integration paradigm facilitates precisely such formulations of national chauvinism.

To be sure, a critique of the integration paradigm is nothing new. By the early 2000s, it had already crystallized around the concept of *inclusion* (Czollek et al., "Radical Diversity"). While integration demanded the assimilation of those who needed to be integrated, inclusion focused on altering society in order to facilitate participation. This shift in focus also manifested itself in legislation. In 2001, a quota was introduced requiring companies to show proof that at least five percent of their personnel were people with disabilities—or else pay a fine. States and municipalities were provided funding to ensure that workplaces were (re)built with better accessibility. And these were great updates. At the same time, the inclusion approach failed to extend the logic of participation to a critical rethinking of the very structures of discrimination. De-integration, on the other hand, isn't only about asking how certain groups can be more or less well integrated into the existing society, but rather, how *society* itself can come to be recognized as *a place of radical diversity*.

In today's Germany, approximately a quarter of the population has something that bureaucratic language calls *Migrationshintergrund*—a migration history, or a family history of migration. Half of these residents also possess a German passport. And this trend is increasing. In the face of such statistics, it requires a grotesque rejection of reality to continue maintaining that one only qualifies as German if one follows the model of an alleged German guiding culture. A diversity of desires, ideologies, and migration (hi)stories has long since become the norm in Germany. It is Germany's political concepts that have lagged behind. Or that have, perhaps, purposely endeavored to resist Germany's diversity. De-integration is grounded in this reality of social diversity— from ideology to sexuality and everywhere in between. This doesn't merely correspond to social reality, but also to German history. Because with the exception of a long decade between the early 1930s and the mid-1940s, Germany was never a monocultural society. Against the claims of one dominant culture, de-integration posits a strategy of conscious refusal to integrate. And this refusal to play along creates room for new perspectives.

Independent of this de-integration concept, I want to underline that the question of whether someone wants to "live near or contrary to us" has nothing to do with whether they are German or not. Not to mention their right to live in Germany. This is an essential aspect of our right to freedom in a democracy. So, even if you're not on board with my concept of de-integration, it is part of our shared democratic responsibility to oppose any group that claims the right to decide who belongs in this country and who doesn't. Because we're all still here: Muslims, Queers, Jews, urban nihilists, secularists, and Pastafarians of the Church of the Flying Spaghetti Monster. We don't just merely *want* to live in a different society. We already do. And we won't be subdued so easily by the pretensions and desires of German dominant culture.

And, if I haven't gotten this point across already, let me provide one final line of summary: Those who dream of a Germany without Muslims, also dream of a Germany without Jews.

5

THAT GERMAN DESIRE: ON THE FUNCTION OF THE JEWS

THE HÖCKES AND KUBITSCHEKS, the von Storchs and Gaulands of this world may be foolish, but they are no fools. And so they have all decided to position themselves—rhetorically speaking—on the side of the Jews. Regardless of whether their claims align with their actions. The AfD is a friend of the Jews: *Jawohl!* And it seems there are at least a few Jews who are friends of the AfD, as well. We published an analysis of this development by Micha Brumlik in the first issue of *Jalta*, a magazine on the Jewish contemporary for which I am co-editor. The whole thing is absurd, and yet the way in which the AfD appropriates Germany's Jews (along with the way some of them allow themselves to be appropriated) is merely the pinnacle of the greater symbolic charge that the existence of living Jews provides the German Theater of Memory. For years now, Germans on all sides of the political spectrum have developed strategies for tethering Jews within the framework of their own expectations and desires—while disregarding any potential feedback or interference.

The various representatives of the German position usually fail to recognize this inner continuity between them—they are much too busy pointing out those things that make them different. Righty vs. spritey Germany. East vs. West is only the tip of the iceberg. Jews play the extras in this negotiation. I've already spoken of President Richard von Weizsäcker's instrumentalization of Jewish tradition. The reinvention of Germany's self-image as the liberated Germans culminated in a victim-centered—in this case the Jewish victim—policy of *Vergangenheitsbewältigung*. This interpretation of overcoming the past has become the dominant expression of Germany's politics of memory. The functionalization of Jewish positionalities is the norm for this country—one need only look or listen a bit more carefully. And so I've dedicated this chapter to examples of the kinds of functionalization I've come across through my own engagements with German literature and in the process of my own literary work.

In 1959, *Münchner Merkur* published a review of the works of Jewish poet Nelly Sachs titled "Die Steine der Freiheit" [Stones of Freedom] by the preeminent young intellectual Hans Magnus Enzensberger (Adorno, "Prismen," 30). In his childhood, Enzensberger had been expelled from the Hitler Youth as a troublemaker, and he ascended to become a figurehead for the German Left over the decades that followed.

He begins his text with reference to Theodor W. Adorno's 1951 dictum that it would be barbaric to write poetry after Auschwitz. The Jewish philosopher had wanted to argue that—after the Shoah—poetry writing can no longer be viewed as an innocent activity. Enzensberger, on the other hand, wanted to overcome this issue, and so he writes:

> If we wish to go on living, this statement must be exonerated. Few have accomplished this. Nelly Sachs is one of them. Her language contains something of salvation in it. In speaking, she gives us back—sentence by sentence—something that we had feared to lose: language itself. (772)

While antisemites desire to remove Jews from their thoughts and lifeworlds entirely in order to construct their own self-image, Enzensberger instead endows the Jewish perspective with a quality of salvation. For Enzensberger, the Jewish poet Nelly Sachs fulfills a dual function: She empowers the community of German perpetrators to return to their language, while her own language offers these same perpetrators salvation by sanctioning their existence on a cultural level. The idea of a kind of catharsis for the Germans through the Jews is a favorite for left-leaning, postwar German intellectuals. It is also an elegant solution by which one does not need to reject Adorno's sentiment about the impossibility of innocent art after Auschwitz directly. One can, instead, simply harness it toward their own hope for relief. And so, Enzensberger goes on to describe Nelly Sachs as follows:

> Her work does not contain one single word of hatred: the hangmen and everything else that renders us their confidants and accomplices are granted neither threat nor forgiveness. They receive no curse, no retribution. There is no language for them. The poems speak instead of those with human faces: the victims.

It is no coincidence that this reading represents the opposite of that antisemitic trope of the vengeful Jew. Instead, Nelly Sachs is allocated a prodigious—almost sacred—task that need have nothing to do with her actual intentions: She becomes a servant of her German commentator. She is declared a symbol of German salvation after Auschwitz. It is unsurprising, then, that Enzensberger regards Sachs not firstly as a poet, but as a victim. And this legacy continues up to the present day. When Jewish people make art, Germans believe it is intended for them as Germans. Just ask any Jewish artist. They will confirm.

Here's one example from my own daily grind: A little while back, I sat at a podium in Berlin alongside a former council president of Germany's Evangelical Church. We talked about this and that, and eventually, we came to the topic of Martin Luther and the question of whether the Evangelical Church could today engage in a "Jewish-Christian dialog" despite its own antisemitic tradition. Toward the end of this discussion, the former council president took the mic and commented: We need your Jewish perspective to critique Martin Luther! Yeah, I believe it. But I'd call that a service. And for services, there are providers who typically receive payment for their labor. And I don't work in this sector. I don't want to save Germany's churches. I really don't.

The functionalization of the Jewish position—which ultimately aims for an amalgamation of the discourse around German exoneration—renders any uniquely specific aspects of the Jewish perspective invisible. It's an act of appropriation by someone like Enzensberger to claim that Nelly Sachs' poetry sought to provide relief or empowerment for the Germans vis-à-vis their own ability to speak. It's an act of appropriation when Joachim Gauck claimed that the Jews were "a gift for us Germans" on International Day of Holocaust Remembrance 2015. Jewish people are not a gift. Certainly not for the Germans. And they are not here *for*, but rather *despite* the Germans and their history. Because they want to be a part of this country. The former German president's gratitude is an expression of the same narcissistic self-confidence with which some Germans assume that their desire for normalization represents a universal need. Except that it's not universal. Even after Auschwitz, the story doesn't only revolve around the German perpetrators. Sorry: not sorry.

There are many different motivations for appropriating Jewish perspectives—and surprisingly, spite and malice play only a small role in this. Maybe you haven't noticed yet, but old-fashioned antisemitism isn't the primary topic of this book. The main focus, instead, is Germany's fixation on its own crimes: something my aunt calls the "ongoing fantasy of omnipotence" [*fortgesetzte Allmachtsphantasie*]. The flipside of this narcissistic fixation is an all-encompassing ignorance on the part of German critics when it comes to recognizing (neve rmind discussing) the complexity of contemporary Jewish experiences, feelings, and positionalities. The way these might, for example, be expressed through art. As a German, the principal thing you know about the Jews is that you killed them. As a consequence, non-Jewish Germans tend to lose sight of the real, extant Jewish people living in Germany today. This ignorance is further maintained through the fear that real Jewish people might be less friendly, less happy, or less forgiving than one might hope (and need) in order to go on speaking German and living in Germany in good conscience. Enzensberger's interpretation of Nelly Sachs' poems as not containing "one single word of hatred [. . .] no curse, no retribution" illustrates this swimmingly.

This is why, in the Theater of Memory, the Good German needs the *Good* Jew as counterpart—a figure so saccharine sweet that one could never imagine them containing even a single drop of unforgiveness in their veins. Of course, there are stories of evil, angry, hateful Jewish people who didn't want reconciliation but revenge after 1945—Jewish people who exercised their need for revenge in various ways. These stories are simply seldom told. But traces of such counternarratives can be found in the works of Paul Celan, Rose Ausländer, or even Nelly Sachs—although these authors have by and large been canonized by German literary critics (along with the general German public) as Good Jews. I'll be discussing the history of Jewish revenge in greater detail a little later. But you can already begin your joyful anticipation now.

During the first decades after 1945, Jews played the role of saviors of the German language and German culture for that German *we* in the Theater of Memory: "the hangmen and everything else that renders us their confidants and accomplices." Following 1968, their function began to transform because Germany's (not-so-)collective *we* stopped understanding itself as a hangman and began, increasingly, to conceptualize itself as a fellow victim: The Germans weren't defeated, they were liberated. This development culminated after Reunification in a new historical narrative. If Germany's relationship to Jews had previously revolved around reconciliation between victims and perpetrators, the Theater of Memory began—increasingly—to concentrate on a narrative of shared retrospection and shared horror. People began to identify with the Jewish victims and their experiences.

A more contemporary example of this phenomenon is the poem "Und es war ein Tag" [And It Was a Day] by the poet Nora Gomringer.

Nora Gomringer was uniquely present in 2017 due to the controversy around the poem "avenidas" by her father, Eugen Gomringer—a poem that students campaigned to have removed from the wall of their university in Berlin. But the present focus isn't on that particular incident, but rather on the larger social relevance poetry may assume. Nora Gomringer was born in 1980, and has led the Künstlerhaus Villa Concordia in Bamberg since 2010. She is indisputably one of the most visible poets of her generation. In 2015, she received the Ingeborg Bachmann Prize, one of the highest honors granted for German-language literature. Already in 2012, she was awarded the city of Cuxhaven's prestigious Joachim Ringelnatz Prize: the subject of my present critique. The jury for this prize was overwhelmingly composed of literary scholars. And during the award ceremony, Gomringer's poem "Und es war ein Tag" received particular acknowledgment. The poem begins as follows:

And it was a day
And the day was ending
And it was standing and it was waiting
And it was a crowd and it looked like a sea
And it was men and it was women

And it was children and it smelled like leather
And it was suitcases and it was steaming
And it was mouths and it was the word
And it was toneless and it was numb
And it was great and it was coats
And it was dogs and it was whimpering
And it was weeping and it was a train
And it was train cars and it was a ramp
And it was bustling and the cry: Inside

The poem continues for a while in similar fashion. I'm going to interrupt here and just skip to the end:

And it was shreds and it was words
And it surely was not true
And it was a shock
And it was true
And it was a strange name
Au-schw-itz

Raise your hand if you were surprised by that ending. It was all already clear as day for me after I read the words "train cars" and "ramp." Why? Because these words belong to the pop-cultural archive of the Shoah. It might leave a bitter taste in your mouth, but it's hard to argue away: Fiddles and suitcases, trains and ramps are *the* images that come to mind when we think about the Holocaust. This poem revolves entirely within the framework of these primary associations: Holocaust kitsch. But this isn't about critiquing the poem itself. I'm far more interested in the jury's justification for awarding Gomringer their prize: that Gomringer is one of the best poets of the twentieth and twenty-first centuries *particularly* because of her poem "Und es war ein Tag." It is "the perfect poem." Her commendation ends with the words: "What remains is pure elation at the power of poetry."

Aha. In the poem "Und es war ein Tag," the lyrical I invites the reader to come along on the train ride to Auschwitz. And the jury endorsed this identificatory work of memory with open arms by upholding it as the poet's most exemplary work. This commendation reveals a new type of access to the past that becomes freed—in an absolutely astonishing manner—from one's own positionality. Back in 1959, this would have been unthinkable even for Hans Magnus Enzensberger—which is why he has to make recourse to the Jewish poet Nelly Sachs in order to absolve the German public from their hangman role and give them back their language. Today's German critics, on the other hand, no longer seem to have any problem at all with Germany's crimes. These days, the German jury boards the train to Auschwitz right alongside the Jews.

To provide a bit of contrast to the praise received for the lyrical identification in Gomringer's "Und es war ein

Tag," we might look at Gruppe 47's[*] reaction to Paul Celan's "Todesfuge" [Deathfugue]. After receiving an invitation from Hans Werner Richter, Celan presented his poem in 1952 at the group's tenth meeting in the coastal resort town of Niendorf. The poem's very delivery was disrupted by laughter and agitation. Participants cried out comments like: "That's like the singsong in a synagogue!" or "He sounds like Goebbels when he reads!" (Böttiger, "Die Wahrheit"). To put it mildly: Members of Gruppe 47 reacted with an utter lack of understanding for the emotional reading of this Jewish author's text—although this did not prevent them from ultimately awarding him third place out of the twenty writers presenting at the meeting. This distinction has lent support to later critics such as Helmut Böttiger, who reject the notion that members of Gruppe 47 were antisemitic. I don't really have a problem with that. It's completely irrelevant for my argument whether Hans Werner Richter, who compared Celan's presentation style to Goebbels' that evening around the dinner table, Walter Hilsbecher, who had to read "Todesfuge" a second time due to the uproarious laughter at the initial reading, or one-time (albeit short) card-carrying Nazi Party member Walter Jens, who recounted the event in 1976, were antisemites or not.

---

[*] Gruppe 47 was an informal association of postwar German-speaking writers initiated by Hans Werner Richter.

You don't have to be an outright antisemite still to enjoy the Theater of Memory.

And again: These poems themselves are not essential to my argument, but rather the difference between past and present critics and their reception of poetry. While yesterday's critics reacted with alienation and uncomprehending malice, today's critics react by appropriating the Jewish perspective as their own.

Italian semiotician and author Umberto Eco has argued on numerous occasions that fictions beget their own credibility—plausibilities that are first internalized and then forgotten (182–83). If you watch a few films and read a few books that describe how lizard people rule the world, future reports on lizard overlords might then become more plausible. I would hazard that the jury for the Joachim Ringelnatz Prize was subject to a similar fallacy. They celebrated the "perfection" of a poem's lyrical presentation of the Shoah that was, in reality, comprised entirely of the banal conventions of well-established Holocaust iconography. And in *this* sense, "Und es war ein Tag" truly is the perfect poem: the perfect poem for the present stage of the Theater of Memory. It permits the German reader an unequivocal identification with the deported. I pose the awarding of the Joachim Ringelnatz Prize—accompanied by the explicit reference to this poem—as evidence for the way in which identification with the Jewish victims has evolved to become the central tenet of German memory culture. It has, in fact, become such a matter of course these days that one hardly notices it at all.

Now, I don't want to pretend that Jewish people are completely innocent when it comes to this current state of affairs. Quite the contrary. They have—at times reluctantly, but, more often than not, quite willingly—played along with the roles assigned to them in the Theater of Memory. During the course of this roleplay, the demands of German dominant culture have become intertwined in numerous ways with Jewish self-perception. Talk about antisemitism, brothers and sisters: Let's become Jews! This is bad enough on its own, for it means that our concept of Jewishness develops vis-à-vis German expectations. But it also has consequences for Jewish art, particularly when this art conforms above all to German expectations and German viewing patterns. We might not even need the "perfect poem" about deportation: The work of Jewish artists often already suffices. This could be observed in the exhibition "Vot ken you mach" [What can you do] that ran from December 2013 through May 2014 in the Kunsthaus Dresden. Twenty-four young Jewish artists were asked to respond to the question: Who are you? Only two of their contributions extended beyond the three coordinates of antisemitism, Shoah, and Israel.

Naturally, this tendency to adopt the German perspective can be observed outside the realm of artistic works as well. In July 2015, the most widely circulating German-Jewish newspaper, *Jüdische Allgemeine*, published the headline "Unser Sommermärchen" [Our Summer's Tale]. Crowning this article by Roy Rajber was an image of the fourteenth Maccabiah Games—a Jewish international sporting event that has been organized within the Zionist movement since the 1930s. In 2015, some events were held in Berlin's Olympic Stadium. For those of you who don't know, a "summer's [fairy] tale" is a reference to the euphoria around the 2006 World Cup. But if this wasn't plain enough for German readers, it was hammered in on the third page of the newspaper: a large photo of a stage. In the background—*Achtung!*—a German flag in the shape of the Star of David. Above it, the title: "Was für ein Symbol!" [What a symbol!] (Goldman, 3)—a citation of the opening speech by patron and President Joachim Gauck, who had been overjoyed that this Jewish sporting event could take place in the old Nazi stadium.

When I call for Jewish people to de-integrate, this doesn't mean I want to make discussion of the Shoah, antisemitism, or Israel taboo. Instead, I want to inspire some reflection about the ways in which these topics have become clichés for Jewish representation in Germany: the extent to which our own relationship with these things has come to correspond to German desires. Celan's "Todesfuge" in Niendorf in 1952, Nelly Sachs' "Die Steine der Freiheit" according to Hans Magnus Enzensbergers' interpretation in 1959, a jury's celebration of a Holocaust poem in 2012, and a conversation about Luther with a representative of the Evangelical Church in 2016 are all examples of the various ways in which Jewish authors and Jewish stories are instrumentalized for the revolving stage of the German Theater of Memory. On the other hand, Jewish people have also made the most of their role as mere statistics—celebrating this "better" Germany in which they can experience their own summer's fairy tale or publicly proclaim their fear of Islam (as did the President of the Central Council of Jews in Germany in 2018, when he demanded that Germany revoke the residency permits of all antisemitic migrants) (*Jüdische Allgemeine*, "Entzug"). There is no doubt that the Theater of Memory has earned the qualifying adjective "German-Jewish."

And why not? Michal Bodemann writes in his study of the Theater of Memory that it is an illusion "to believe that Jews live in a ghetto of media deprivation and are not also molded by the currents of German politics and culture" (*Gedächtnistheater*, 54). And so Jewish people have come to be every bit as foolish as the Germans. Surprise! And their reasons are every bit as convincing as those of the German playwrights who compose their roles for the Theater of Memory. When the Second World War ended, there was, in fact, debate among Jewish people around an adequate response to the Shoah. In both Germanies, a reconciliatory response quickly established itself as the norm among many

Jewish people—a tradition that continues today. This orientation toward German society was also the result of German Jews' relative isolation from global networks of Jewish people after 1945. Those who remained stranded in Germany after the Shoah—whether due to familial, medical, or other necessities—had a difficult time. They lived under the heavy pressure of constant justification.

Far be it from me to pass judgment on these people. De-integration from German society was not nearly as feasible an alternative seventy, fifty, or even just thirty years ago as it is today. It would not only have required the individual fearlessness that Jewish people also possessed in those days, but also the sheer size and diversity of the Jewish population that first returned to Germany after the 1990s. It was only through this demographic shift that decoupling from the pervasive German positionality became possible. Today, it is no longer essential to forge an alliance with a memory-keen segment of the German population. Which, of course, does not mean that such alliances should no longer be pursued. It simply means that *we* no longer *need* them for our own social survival. And so we reach a critical moment where we can ask ourselves: Why do we continue to play along?

The question of social survival in postwar German society is only one side of the coin. It is every bit as important to consider that Jewish identification with German nationalism is also an expression of that same hope for an ultimate, successful German-Jewish symbiosis that was pervasive in German Jewry before National Socialism. This German-Jewish nationalism was so strong, in fact, that it provided impetus to hold the first Zionist Congress in 1897 in Basel, Switzerland, instead of Munich. The production around the Maccabiah Games in 2015 demonstrates the extent to which many Jewish people today retain this yearning to identify with Germany. German U-boats for Israel! Jewish support for Germany! Historian Dan Diner has described the post-National Socialist proximity between Germans and Jews as "negative symbiosis"—a concept with which he attempts to capture both sides' shared reference of the Shoah. But when I read in the *Jüdische Allgemeine* about "our summer's tale," the negativity seems increasingly to have retreated into the background. What remains is a German flag emblazoned with the Star of David.

I think this kind of cooperation with the German Theater of Memory is a mistake. Even before the War, Jewish people in Germany had already failed in their hope of establishing a German-Jewish symbiosis. And German society canceled their subscription to Jewishness (at the latest) with the murder of six million Jewish people. I think it's past time to move on from this symbiosis project. And to end the chapter on an even more unconciliatory note than my non-fiction repertoire allows, I'd like to cite an excerpt from my 2017 play *Celan mit der Axt* [Celan with the Axe], instead. In the following passage, the fictional Jewish character Amichai Süß muses on the topic of revenge:

> Sometimes I really ask myself whether the Germans think we're stupid, or whether they simply think that they could get off so easily. First exterminate six million people and afterward establish a couple monuments and holidays and roll out a few million euros for survivors and then: *Bam—no hard feelings!* And you know, the worst thing about it might be that it worked! Just look at the schmucks leading our Jewish congregations today. One could almost think the Holocaust was just some kind of integration scheme. Project objectives achieved! Moses Mendelssohn is dancing in his grave! Old Lady Varnhagen is clapping her sweaty little hands in joy. But we're not you're Good Victims, we're the evil ones. We're not reasonable. I don't even know what reasonable means.

6

WOWSCHWITZ, OR: CAN WE LAUGH ABOUT AUSCHWITZ?

ON JANUARY 28, 2016, ARD* moderator Anja Reschke commented on the recently established International Day of Holocaust Remembrance. Toward the end of her televised, two-minute address for a program commemorating the anniversary of the liberation of Auschwitz, Reschke observes the following:

> I belong to the third generation. I wasn't there. And yet, I still felt ashamed when I saw the images. Because this is a part of my identity as a German, whether I want it to be or not. After watching the film, I couldn't sleep. And so, I channel-surfed. And what did I see? A PEGIDA demonstration in Dresden protesting the presence of immigrants in Germany. And I have to say: That's when I truly felt sick.

---

* *Arbeitsgemeinschaft der öffentlich-rechtlichen Rundfunkanstalten der Bundesrepublik Deutschland* [Working Group of Public Broadcasters of the Federal Republic of Germany].

In the hours that followed, Reschke's commentary became an object of heated debates, particularly in Facebook feeds, on Twitter, and in the comment sections on the ARD website. Reschke's enthusiastic supporters clashed with reactionary rejections that read like a model study for the deflection of guilt: What's that got to do with us? Why should I be ashamed of my history? Israel's doing the same thing in Gaza! This kind of argument just oppresses German people!

And so on. And so forth.

The combat formations remain clearly delineated and familiar: On one side, the servants of the public media provide a loudspeaker for the narrative of the liberated German victims in the tradition of Weizsäcker. On the other side, those who reject the centrality of Holocaust memory in the German present as a "cult of guilt" or a state religion have coalesced around movements and parties like PEGIDA and the AfD. But January 27, 2016, also proved to be a productive anniversary in other ways when it came to writing this book. In the days leading up to the International Day of Holocaust Remembrance, the ARD had promoted their evening program for the anniversary with announcements published in the digital and print editions of *Frankfurter Allgemeine Zeitung*, *ZEIT*, and *Spiegel*. Their graphics depicted a barbwire fence, a few chimneys in the twilight, and beneath them, the lines:

#AUSCHWITZ

FOR ME IS: _____.

Beneath this was a broad field of darkness, followed by the additional lines:

The ARD Program Focus for the 70th Anniversary
of the Liberation of Auschwitz
I'm headed for Auschwitz—Today at 10:45 PM

Night Will Fall—Today at 11:30 PM.

When a friend showed me this advertisement on his phone, I had to laugh. What did I find so amusing, you ask? Pretty much everything. Firstly: the picture's romantic aesthetics. Then the capital letters of the title: #AUSCHWITZ. Was the hashtag meant to anticipate the fuzzy barbwire that remained visible just behind the headline? Concrete poetry? But no, obviously, the title "#Auschwitz for me is: _____" was about completing (and proliferating) the message over the social media platform Twitter. What better compliment than the television program's advertisement: "I'm headed for Auschwitz." Wow. I can hardly imagine a better invitation for self-identification. And to think: I thought the poem "Und es war ein Tag" was crass.

In the previous chapter, I described how Germany's *dispositif* of memory has displayed an increasing tendency toward identification with the (Jewish) victims over the course of the last decades. A more detailed study of this phenomenon can be read in the 2010 *Gefühlte Opfer* [Perceived Victims] by historian Ulrike Jureit and psychoanalyst Christian Schneider. Their study also examines the Holocaust Memorial in Berlin, whose architect, Peter Eisenman, once proclaimed that it should also transmit the feeling of the gas chamber to a Japanese tourist. Ultimately, the things an architect says about their work are irrelevant. What *is* interesting, however, is that the Bundestag decided to go with his design. Jureit and Schneider observe: "The second generation chose an architectural simulation of death in Auschwitz for symbolic expression, and manifested with this the whole potential for downplaying and denial that accompanied their victim identification-based concept of remembrance" (29). Obviously, the very notion of Shoah reenactment is utterly preposterous. No one will *ever* feel like they're in a gas chamber unless they're actually *in* a gas chamber. Something I hope none of us will ever experience. *Bezrat Hashem*.

Discussions that preceded the official 2005 opening of this monument also revolved around the question: Just who is this place really for? It quickly transpired that the Germans wanted to build a monument for themselves. And that's OK. Jewish people will remember this history anyway. Former Chancellor Gerhard Schröder even described the Holocaust Memorial as "a place one likes to visit" [*ein Ort, an den man gerne geht*] (which is also the title of a volume documenting the discussions leading up to the monument by political scientist

Claus Leggewie and cultural scientist Erik Meyer). At first glance, this statement might be irritating—after all, we *are* talking about a place to remember six million murdered Jewish people. But it also makes sense when one considers how the memory of this genocide helped found a new German sense of community. Consequently, Maxim Biller deems the murder of Jewish people in his 1996 essay "Heiliger Holocaust" [Holy Holocaust] the "mother, at long last, of an invented German national identity" and describes the monument as a temple erected for this Holy Mother.

The thesis of identifying with the Jewish victims corresponds with the findings of the 2002 *Opa war kein Nazi* [Grandpa Wasn't a Nazi] by sociologists Harald Welzer, Sabine Moller, and Karoline Tschuggnall, which investigates the development of a familial narrative of memory across three generations. According to the authors, the silence of the first generation was followed by a distancing from National Socialism in the second generation—the 68ers. The third generation continued this development by construing a memory of victimhood in which the Nazis in their own families were recast as victims or as heroes—thus the title of the work: Grandpa wasn't a Nazi. This kind of national self-valorization was also mirrored in the design of the memorial. Far-seeing critics like the publicist Eike Geisel had already recognized this connection between self-valorization on a national level and the adaptation of victim and resistance narratives back in the 1980s.

The increasing German identification with victimhood was confirmed in February 2018 by the study *MEMO Deutschland— Multidimensionaler Erinnerungsmonitor* [MEMO Germany— Multidimensional Memory Display], compiled by scholar Andreas Zick at the Institute for Interdisciplinary Research on Conflict and Violence at the University of Bielefeld, alongside psychologist Jonas Rees, working in cooperation with the Berlin Foundation Remembrance, Responsibility, and Future. In a telephone survey conducted among more than 1,000 randomly selected households across Germany, 69 percent of correspondents claimed their families had not been perpetrators during World War II. 18 percent admitted their family's complicity. 12 percent responded that they didn't know. This means, according to their own family (hi)stories, that more than two-thirds of the Germans weren't Nazis. Even if we consider the possibility that a number of the correspondents were recent immigrants, this still reflects an ahistorically high number. Which means that official memories provide no guarantee of personal memories. On the contrary: The official staging of remembrance serves, instead, as a ritual of exoneration when it comes to familial guilt. One more generation, and there won't have been a single Nazi in the German family tree.

Germany isn't doing away with itself;* instead, it's doing away with its memory of perpetrating the crimes of World

---

* A reference to the controversial title *Deutschland schafft sich ab* [Germany Is Doing Away with Itself] by Thilo Sarrazin. For a more detailed discussion, see Chapter 7.

War II. And in the process, it's reinventing its own self-image to identify increasingly with the victims of National Socialism. This is not a sudden development, but rather the product of a continual negotiation of the German self-image. The current status of this debate can easily be identified in the latest films produced by the public media channels. The three-part 2013 kitsch production *Unsere Mütter, unsere Väter* [Our Mothers, Our Fathers; English title: *Generation War*] presents the Nazi time as a period of shared suffering and remembrance. It tells the story of five friends persecuted by the Nazi regime— among them the Jewish character, Viktor. None of these five characters is a Nazi, and the Jew, Viktor, is of course a complex figure with his own angels and demons: an everyman caught up in an age of extremes. War is bad for everyone.

The question of *German* self-conception is the driving force behind all debates around political remembrance in this country. Time and again, the Holocaust Memorial turns up center-stage in those discussions. Just remember January 2017, when AfD politician Björn Höcke described it to his followers in Dresden as a "monument of shame." Now, I've already pointed to the continuities between this description and Martin Walser's acceptance speech for the Peace Prize nearly twenty years earlier. It was therefore not particularly innovative for Höcke to describe Germany as the "only nation in the world" to "erect a *monument of shame* in the heart of its capital city." And it's not important to me whether he's referring here to the monument or the Holocaust as shameful. His point is that those people whom he considers to be the German nation can only perceive their history in a negative light. And to counter this, he calls for "a cultural memory that exposes those things and those great accomplishments of our forebears." Yeah, OK. Right. That's definitely a problem Jewish people in Germany don't have.

But in January 2017, the standard public debate around current German self-conception progressed slightly differently. A few days after Höcke's speech, the Jewish satirist Shahak Shapira launched his online project yolocaust.de—a project denouncing the behavior of a certain subset of Holocaust Memorial visitors. The hashtag #yolocaust had already existed before Shapira's project: employed mostly alongside selfies taken by younger visitors to the Holocaust Memorial. The term was a neologism comprising the word "Holocaust" and the English acronym "YOLO" (you only live once). If the visitor hovered their mouse over the collection of selfies Shapira had harvested from social media users, these pictures revealed photographs of dead or imprisoned Jewish people from the Second World War. In an introductory text, the satirist promised to erase the public display of these selfies from his website as soon as the users apologized for their conduct.

Now, one must acknowledge that Shapira's intervention provided an attempt to appropriate this non-Jewish monument from a Jewish perspective. Shapira's act was an attempt to actively participate in a determination of behavioral norms at the Holocaust Memorial. Respect. This, at the very least, was a fresh take. And the website experienced a largely positive reception in the German feuilletons and international press. But there was also a problem with his concrete realization. Jewish commentators criticized the sensationalized use of photographs: mountains of corpses and crowds of the dying. The tasteless arrangement of pictures on a website and Shapira's own implied, moralistic self-valorization (Funk, "Leichenberge"; Belkin, "Yolocaust"). Particularly in regards to this final point, author Mirna Funk correctly identifies his as an expression of a blatantly German, sacralizing, and unironic approach to the Shoah. And this should not have surprised Shapira, either. After all, the subtitle of his own book, *Das wird man ja wohl noch schreiben dürfen!* [Of Course You Can Still Write This!] describes him as "The Most German Jew in the World."

Of course, there are alternatives to this kind of highly localized, subjective way of relating to the Shoah. Anyone who's heard an Israeli Holocaust joke or watched a Jewish-American television show knows that. Shapira—who was himself born in Israel and spent a good part of his life in other corners of the world—is well aware of this. He, too, is likely familiar with the 2010 YouTube video *Dancing Auschwitz* by Australian artist Jane Korman—a video in which she, her sisters, and her father

Adam "Adolek" Kohn dance to the hit song "I Will Survive" in front of various concentration camps. The video went viral. The distance between dancing in front of a concentration camp and criticizing selfies tagged #yolocaust is every bit as wide as the gap between the triumph of a survivor family and the unreflected actions of a tourist at the Holocaust Memorial. This sort of penal action on Shapira's part thus had to assume that the young people he attacked were not the grandchildren of survivors themselves. He would know that this kind of #yolocaust humor can also score points, especially in the Jewish world. On August 30, 2017, Shapira himself tweeted in response to the comments of another user: "The train to Auschwitz takes me further than your tweets" [*Der Zug nach Auschwitz holt mich mehr ab als deine Tweets*].

Recently, I took part in a conversation at the Deutsches Theater in Göttingen after a staging of George Tabori's *Mein Kampf*. The event was titled: "Darf man über Auschwitz lachen?" [Can We Laugh About Auschwitz?], and the moderator's first question was: "Are we—as the descendants of the perpetrators—allowed to laugh about Auschwitz?" A meister stroke: With a single question, she had initiated the roleplay between Germans and Jews. And I was the Jew, tasked with passing judgment over laughter or non-laughter. I find this demand for Jewish permission ludicrous; I mean, really, who's ever heard of Germans not doing anything because Jews didn't grant them permission? And, you know, this wasn't really a question of anyone prohibiting anything anyway. By asking this question, the moderator simply transformed our conversation after the play into the next episode of the never-ending Telenovela of Memory. Buchenwald Street instead of *Lindenstraße*,[*] but the same level of plot predictability. The Good Germans wanted to ask questions they already knew the answers to. And the Good Jews should tell them again anyway.

Back then, in Göttingen, I considered for a moment whether I should intervene with a de-integrative escalation, but I decided to wait it out, instead. I told the moderator that it depended on the joke. And then someone in the audience stood up and cried out indignantly: "*I*, for one, could *never* laugh about Auschwitz!" Of course not. And then, I responded with my own favorite Holocaust joke:

> Two Holocaust victims are sitting on a cloud and laughing. God comes by and asks: "What are you two laughing about?" The first Jew answers: "Why, about our time in Auschwitz, of course!" To which God replies: "Auschwitz!? But that wasn't funny!" And the second Jew says: "Ah, you wouldn't understand. You just had to be there!"

---

[*] A reference to a popular, long-running German soap opera set on a fictional 'Linden Street' in Munich. Lindenstraße 54 in Potsdam, however, was—like Buchenwald—the location of a forced-labor camp under National Socialism.

And the entire room erupted into laughter. It shook with it. Some of the audience had tears in their eyes when they came to the front to shake my hand. Thank you, thank you. Some threw flowers, some wanted me to autograph their forearms. I could have sworn that someone tried to sneak off after plucking out one of my hairs. Oy, this Jewish humor! It's so nice how they can still make light of it . . . But of course, that's not what happened at all. The serious answer to the question of asking permission to laugh about Auschwitz is: Auschwitz means different things to different people. Some people were interned there; very, very few of them survived. Others worked there as guards. Some people are the children and grandchildren of those imprisoned there. Others are recent immigrants who stand open-mouthed in disbelief before the ovens on school field trips. And many, many, many more are the descendants of the perpetrators and accomplices. People who then—as now—knew nothing about it. And it is *this* fundamental difference of experience that Anja Reschke underscored in her commentary on the ARD that I quoted above.

The Theater of Memory is staged by and for the Germans. On the one hand, those like Reschke remain willing to remember—descendants with the best intentions, conscious of their history, and vehemently ready to support and defend responsible labors of remembrance. And I respect that. On the other hand, Höcke and the New Right reject this practice of remembrance as a cult of guilt in order to reclaim the old

German greatness. I've got no respect for that. But the determining factor in this debate continues to be that both sides are ultimately grappling with the same question: What can and should post-1945 German identity look like? The dominance of this question results in the fact that Jewish people have to align themselves along a German coordinate field whenever they want to talk about the Shoah themselves. And the German staging of the Holocaust typically offers only two options: Either this is our collective memory or we don't want to talk about it. And so the Theater of Memory comes to mean that Jewish memory serves to negotiate German problems.

Today, of course, there are also approaches to remembrance that are not oriented toward a German desire. When the aforementioned Jane Korman danced with her father to Gloria Gaynor's "I Will Survive" before the gates of concentration camps, she was also creating an alternative approach to the subject. Korman's *Dancing Auschwitz* represents an intervention against established viewing patterns by counteracting familiar media representation of concentration camps. The musical selection also gestures toward a sensibility for the commonality of experiences shared by diverse minoritized communities. Cultural scientist Lea Wohl describes this in a 2012 essay:

The dimensions of the struggle against the oppressor and ultimately the victory over and contestation of National

Socialist values is realized through music projected over images: A Jewish Holocaust survivor dances before the crematoriums of Auschwitz to a song by a Black American musician which has become a symbol of the gay rights movement. (187)

This barely four-minute-long video is, in this interpretation, not merely an expression of the triumph of a survivor over those who would have murdered him. It also represents the insecurities of an individual who must first acknowledge and harness his own courage to disrupt taboos: a conquest over the sacrality of transmitted memory.

I predict that this kind of alternative approach will gain traction in Germany, as well, now that those people whose own biographies revolve outside the coordinates of the German-Jewish staging of remembrance have begun to heckle the current personnel at the German Theater of Memory. New figures are making an entry, crying out between the acts and throwing their popcorn at the stage. And in light of these developments, an urgent question arises: How do we sensitize young people (like the selfie-takers of Shapira's intervention) to think beyond currently established questions of identity centered on a German desire for German crimes and Jewish perspectives? Who is to say that #yolocaust could not also represent an alternative approach? Indeed, one of the youths shamed on Shapira's no-longer active website claimed, in his own defense, that he was well known for "punching below the belt." And isn't that how a good Holocaust joke normally works? Its very inappropriateness inspires confusion, discomfort, or even distress among its audience. An apparent lack of respect can also contain contempt for National Socialism, which must be acknowledged alongside the seriousness that a subject like Holocaust remembrance also demands.

Hannah Arendt provides an exemplary illustration of the disruptive power of irony from a Jewish positionality. In her famous conversation with Günter Gaus (a video that has received hundreds of thousands of views on YouTube), the German-Jewish philosopher discusses the often-vehement criticism she received from Jewish commentators regarding the ironic tone of her work *Eichmann in Jerusalem*:

> Some people take it amiss . . . I can understand that to some extent . . . That I can still laugh, for example. But I really thought Eichmann was a fool. I read a transcript of his police hearing. 3600 pages in all, I read it very carefully. I laughed countless times. I laughed out loud. People were offended by this. I can't do anything about that. But I know one thing. I'd probably still laugh three minutes before certain death. That, they say, is the tone of my book. [. . .] The tone is really the person. [. . .] The tone is an objection against me personally. I can't help that.

From a Jewish perspective, the strategy of de-integration means recognizing different positions and different approaches to the German crime. That might be irony, when irony is least expected. And it can be anger or vengefulness where reconciliation and shared memory are expected. De-integration means disrupting the growing tendency of Germans to identify with the Jewish victims. It means making the *German* perspective visible, rather than accepting it as normative—it means thinking beyond a paradigm that alternates between shared remembrance and the denial of history. De-integration positions itself against participation in the Theater of Memory. Maybe we might ride the same train to Auschwitz together, but our paths diverge at the gates. Because it is here that the two parts of the (hi)story have always differed decisively: that of the Germans and that of the Jews. This history should not be confused.

For Jewish people, de-integration also means overcoming the barriers that we so often erect in our own hearts and minds: be it due to our sense of responsibility for the dead or our own deeply held fears that we will not be recognized. That we remain unacknowledged. But the alternative is not this German dichotomy of remembrance or no remembrance, Jews for Germans or not Jewish at all. The alternative is understanding both: laughing and crying, de-integration and Jewish identity. Throw out the fiddles, blow out the candles. Where we're headed, we won't need them anymore.

7

ALTERNATIVES FOR GERMANS: WHAT WE CAN LEARN FROM THE AFD

IN HIS VERY FIRST (if long-awaited) speech on October 3, 2017, President Frank-Walter Steinmeier proclaimed the following: "The lessons of two World Wars, the lessons of the Holocaust, the full rejection of all ethnonationalist [*völkisch*] thinking, racism, and anti-Semitism, as well as assuming responsibility for the security of Israel—all this is part of being German." And there it was again: the good old Weizsäcker tradition. Except that federal parliamentary elections had just taken place nine days before. And in light of the results of those elections, Steinmeier's recourse to this self-image of the Good German came across like a mix between provocation, defiance, and plain old absurdity. Because on September 24, 2017, just under six million adult Germans had voted for *völkisch*-ethnonationalist and anti-pluralist political thought. The claim of an antiracist, anti-antisemitic, and anti-*völkisch*

Germanness had just been radically refuted by recent events. And by that, I don't just mean election results; I also mean the uncovering of the National Socialist Underground (NSU), PEGIDA's Monday demonstrations, the list goes on . . .

Steinmeier's distancing from racist and antisemitic positionalities was accompanied by his silent refusal to acknowledge how election day had made German society's ongoing entanglement with the history of National Socialism visible. Instead, the president stood at his lectern on German Unification Day and acted like this new German "normality" had prevailed and carried on unchanged. It's difficult for me to see anything else in Steinmeier's insistence than the expression of a wish for how Germany *should* be—but isn't, and also never was.

This kind of refusal to recognize political reality is no exception to the rule for German politicians. On December 18, 2017, Anetta Kahane, leader of the Amadeu Antonio Foundation—a prominent organization engaged against racism, rightwing extremism, and antisemitism in Germany—described an episode for the *Frankfurter Rundschau* that had occurred several years earlier during a visit with the Governing Mayor of Berlin:

> Approximately twenty people had come—Berlin Jews: advisers, artists, athletes, students, journalists, business folk. They told stories, one after the other. Every story was

about insults; degradation; forced discussions about guilt, the Holocaust, and wicked Israel; the lack of protection for Jewish children threatened by violence. These stories took place on the street, at university, in school, at youth clubs, at work parties, on the playground, in art galleries or fitness studios. The aggressions had come from every kind of German—mainstream or minority, rightwing or left. After everyone present had spoken, there was a moment of silence in the room. Then the mayor stood up. No, he said, he couldn't believe that. There was no danger of antisemitism, and Jews could move about as freely as they pleased. He took a photo with a Jewish athlete; then he left. Leaving us behind with open mouths.

The mayor left the room because he didn't want to know how normal experiences of antisemitism are. When Steinmeier claimed that "the full rejection of all ethnonationalist thinking, racism, and anti-Semitism" was a part of being German, he ignored one eighth of Germany's voters. At the very minimum. But apparently, the president and mayor alike know more about how Germany *really* is. In their 2017 "primer," *Mit Rechten reden* [Talking with the Right], Per Leo, Maximilian Steinbeis, and Daniel-Pascal Zorn attempt to account for such denials of reality. For these authors, this denial is rooted in a moralism they detect particularly in their "leftist friends" (35–40). I, too, recognize this particular brand of denial, but I think the attempt to locate it politically is nonsense. The denial of reality is not some specific attribute of the political Left, but rather the basis for all German claims of normality—relying, as they do, upon the inversion of relations between self-image and political reality. Because Germans no longer wish to be perceived as *völkisch*, antisemitic, and racist, political reality must behave accordingly. And so the 12.6 percent of the population who voted for the AfD are reframed not as an affirmation of ethnonationalist thinking, but as an expression of "political frustration." And the past continues to be treated as though it were the past. You know: *Vergangenheitsbewältigung* [overcoming the past]. Because things can't come to be, if we don't permit them to.

Alas, if only the president were just speaking strategically in order not to concede discursive space to the Far Right. But I don't think this is very plausible. In preparation for his speech, Steinmeier spent months traveling through Germany to meet people and converse with them. The Republic had been awaiting this hot take on the issue for quite some time. And this speech was the result of his field work. Author and Gorki Theater columnist Mely Kiyak provides the following commentary on Steinmeier's words:

Maybe I'm nuts or something, but I'll try to explain it this way: Uwe Böhnhardt, Uwe Mundlos, and Beate Zschäpe are all picture-perfect examples of people who reject everything that Steinmeier just listed off. They're antisemites, racists, *völkisch*-ethnonationalists, etc. Are people suddenly rejecting their German identity? Are all Germans now antiracists by birth?

Precisely. It's not like Steinmeier could have completely ignored the political Right, but it is revealing how he chose to thematize them. He spoke of new "walls that arise due to alienation, disappointment and anger" in this country, by which he probably sought to describe the motivation behind voters electing the AfD. And that was it. Really. This isn't just paternalistic—in that it fails to seriously reflect on people's political decisions. It also demonstrates Steinmeier's refusal to recognize the AfD as a returning specter of ethnonationalist thinking in this country, and its voters, as the willing enforcers of this movement. As if AfD voters were children who didn't realize the consequences of their actions. Which is total bullshit. Or doesn't matter. Because who'd actually believe that everyone who voted for the NSDAP also subscribed to the *Stürmer* or read Hitler's *Mein Kampf*? Well, the president didn't want to ruminate about this chapter of German history anyway. His interpretation of the political situation relied on a self-image that—as price for his adherence to its vision—left him no other choice but to construe the voters of an openly far-right party as the frustrated portion of an otherwise good, antiracist, and anti-*völkisch* Germany.

One might suppose that such an analysis of the present—grounded in a self-image as the Good German—would receive increasing scrutiny the further the political reality in Germany slips away from its own self-projections. And yet, despite every warning sign (of which the parliamentary election was only the latest and most visible), the anthem of the new, normal, and positively *Heimat*-conscious Germany continues to be sung. I need only say: the Ministry of *Heimat*. Or quote Steinmeier again, when he says: "Those who yearn for *Heimat* are not living in the past."* Apparently the official, political representatives of this country aren't ready to give up satisfying their own nationalistic urges just because a couple Germans took things too far. No one stopped the music when asylum homes started burning over the past few years either.

If you scratch the surface a little, it's easy to see that Steinmeier's use of *Heimat* is anything but unproblematic. After touching on the definition of what constitutes legal migration to Germany, he turns to the subject of the "new arrivals": "This means that those who arrive in our midst must first learn to speak our language, learn about democracy, our Basic Law, history." Steinmeier found it crucial to remind

---

* This translation is my own. The official English translation of his words "I am convinced those who want to feel at home are not stuck in the past" paints a misleading representation of the politicized language of the German original [*Ich bin überzeugt, wer sich nach Heimat sehnt, der ist nicht von gestern*].

us that refugees must kindly behave themselves when they come to Germany. Let's take a minute here: an ethnonationalist, far-right party is inducted into German parliament, and Steinmeier instructs the primary victim group of rightwing violence to integrate. As a refugee, that would sure make me feel welcomed with open arms. And then the president bids members of a "young, optimistic generation" in this country to celebrate German unity. Wait a minute! Is this the same optimistic generation composed—in no small number—by those directly threatened with physical violence by the party platform and beliefs of the AfD? This could at least have been an opportunity to assure refugees, (im)migrants, and their children that the state would provide them protection. But there was no word from Steinmeier about this. Not one single word.

In Mainz, on October 3, 2017, the president made a decision. Would he show solidarity with refugees, (im)migrants, "postmigrants" (as their descendants call themselves here), and Muslims threatened by the rhetorical and physical attacks of a *völkisch*-ethnonationalist political Right? Or would he show solidarity with those who have no problem voting for a party with such a political agenda? The president decided quite clearly to show empathy for the voters—also those voters of the AfD. The benefit of the doubt for an ethnic German community.

*

Like Steinmeier, I've also traveled extensively through this republic since the first appearance of the AfD in state parliaments; to meet people and talk with them. In doing so, I've heard a wide range of explanations for the success of this new party. Some explained to me that it was a protest movement, the result of political frustration. That it wasn't really about concrete political ideology, but mostly about being "antiestablishment." That could have been the case with Hitler, too, I thought, sipping my gin and tonic. I also met with people who saw—in voters of the AfD—lost and disgruntled Germans who could be won back. There was a tenderness in their language that really triggered me. As if we'd neglected to take these people with us on our antiracist and anti-antisemitic field trips.

What exactly would it mean to "take them with" us? And had they even wanted to come along in the first place, when the school bus was waiting, honking at the curb? Did they stick out their thumbs, even a fraction of an inch, when first the Turkish-German and then the postmigrant theater floats paraded by with their confetti cannons? Whenever I heard this mantra on my travels about gathering the lost souls of AfD voters, I felt like standing up, throwing my plastic cup into one of the tidy corners, shaking my counterpart and screaming: Don't you have anything better up your sleeve? Nothing but empathy or shoulder shrugs? The real scandal is that seventy-three years after the end of National Socialism a platform like the AfD's could be acceptable to—electable by—so many people in Germany. It's a catastrophe. CA-TAS-TRO-PHE.

In the past few months, there've also been suggestions on a political level about how to deal with the New Right. The blinders strategy of just ignoring them can probably be dismissed as ineffective after the parliamentary elections. Then, the idea of controlled confrontation suggested in *Mit Rechten reden* à la Per Leo, Maximilian Steinbeis, and Daniel-Pascal Thorn became the vogue. Those who fight their way through the book's fanciful passages—its dizzying metaphors only rendering things more complicated than they are—find this basic recommendation: Argue with the Right as earnestly as you can and let them make themselves laughable on their own. It's important to recognize the distinction that, for the authors, one can only label those as "rightwing" who speak in a specific discursive manner (12). Those who don't speak at all, but simply commit one of the four crimes that—according to the Amadeu Antonio Foundation and Pro Asyl—have been committed, on average, against refugees daily in 2017, well, they don't even pop up on the search radar in the first place. With this, the authors rule out a central tenet of rightwing politics from the get-go: violence. Simply defined away.

The authors of *Mit Rechten reden* already miss the mark in the title of their book: because with the New Right, it's frequently not about an exchange at all, but simply a discursive hegemony. Thor von Waldstein, an author from the rightwing publisher Antaios, calls this strategy *metapolitics*. Ironically, this term can be traced back to the Marxist Italian philosopher Antonio Gramsci, though it's been enjoying tremendous popularity among rightwing intellectuals, as well, since its employment by Alain de Benoist, the instigator behind the Nouvelle Droite in France. In questions of hegemony, the ability to impose one's own topics and interpretations onto others is central. Cogent argumentation can also play a role, but it doesn't have to. In fact, it seems to be irrelevant for most people anyway: those who believe Israel is a hindrance to world peace but still think it's a lovely place for a holiday, those who think a constitutional democracy is important but have no problem when ID numbers are removed from police uniforms, or all those AfD gentlemen demanding social solidarity and economic neoliberalism at the same time. Political opinions aren't based on argumentative consistency—which is why they can't be overcome at this discursive level either. For Leo, Steinbeis, and Zorn, the New Right first and foremost represent a "language game" (28). For me and my friends, they represent the increased potential for physical harm.

The prevailing approach to dealing with the New Right in politics is showing one's understanding for the already proverbial hardships and tribulations of their people. Inevitably, this recognition goes along with the acceptance of certain political principles—the fear of "foreign infiltration" is incomprehensible without an ideal of homogeneity,

Islamophobia without the belief in a German guiding culture. I've got to say: With all this pessimism, I was surprised by the excitement with which so many German politicians and publicists reacted to the electoral success of the AfD. It seemed as though they'd downright been waiting to concede room in their stories, interviews, and opinion pieces for rightwing, ethnonationalist, and liberal-nationalist positions.

A popular example from the time around the parliamentary elections was provided, of course, by Bavaria's Christian Social Union (CSU)—a political party with already nothing to their right but a razor-wire border wall. A party that never tires of surpassing itself in the promotion of backward-facing ideas about innovation. Was it not their very own Franz Josef Strauß who—in fitting celebration of the German economic miracle [*Wirtschaftswunder*]—proclaimed: A nation that has achieved such economic accomplishments has the right to no longer want to hear about Auschwitz? Alexander Dobrindt aligned himself seamlessly with this kind of party thinking when he demanded a new conservative revolution. I've already joked about this in a different chapter, but the consequences of this kind of behavior are not funny at all. If the strategy for winning back rightwing voting groups becomes adopting their rightwing positions, the CSU will soon be so far to the right that they'll eliminate any need for another rightwing party.

The Social Democrats (SPD) may point their political middle fingers at the AfD and PEGIDA, but they continue to deny their own rightward shift.* In 2017, the notoriously shrill (and in the meantime silenced) loudspeaker Sigmar Gabriel formulated his vision of a Social Democratic Party that would no longer need to make taboo such terminology as *Heimat* or *Leitkultur*. A vision that could re-connote these concepts in a positive manner. There is also an exhaustive tribute to *Heimat* in Steinmeier's speech, even if the president represents this idea in a non-partisan manner. Both statements are not exceptions to—but rather the expressions of—a tangible trend. Immediately after their electoral defeat, the influential state association of North Rhine-Westphalia wanted to oversee the transformation of the SPD into a "modern *Heimat* party." Their youth organization objected. All the same: In 2017, Thilo Sarrazin remained a card-carrying member of the SPD—and it's no coincidence that *Spiegel* journalist Melanie Amann begins her book *Angst für Deutschland* [Fear for Germany] about the growing strength of the AfD, with a discussion of Sarrazin's *Deutschland schafft sich ab* [Germany Is Doing Away with Itself].

It doesn't look much better for the Green Party, even if they don't have a figurehead like Sarrazin to trot out. Party chair Katrin Göring-Eckardt announced in October 2017: "We love this country. It's our *Heimat*." She was criticized for

---

* Here the author makes a clever neologism out of the name of the notoriously rightward-leaning SPD politician Thilo Sarrazin.

this by the Green Youth [Grüne Jugend] faction of her party, but nevertheless received support from fellow party members like Cem Özdemir, Reinhard Bütikofer, Robert Habeck, and Renate Künast. I won't even start with populists like Sahra Wagenknecht—she's been brewing her own national and socialist stew within the Left Party [Die Linke] for a while now. And the Free Democrats [FDP] under Christian Lindner promote the selection of refugees according to liberal-economic criteria and the potential for speedy deportation. It seems fitting that the FDP coordinated its monochromatic campaign ads with the Berlin-based agency Heimat. In Austria, *Heimatliebe* [love for the *Heimat*] is also no longer the solitary field of rightwing or conservative parties, but has been ploughed extensively by the embattled Green Party presidential candidate Alexander Van der Bellen with slogans like "If you love our *Heimat* don't divide it" or "*Heimat* needs cohesion."

Representatives of all parties active on the federal level in Germany tapped into the same keg in reaction to the AfD—a keg whose murky contents can be summed up with the following statement: We've got to take the concerns of AfD voters seriously. All parties seem to have taken note that successful politics can be made under the banner of *völkisch*-ethnonationalist slogans again. And so they play along. As a consequence, they're reproducing *Heimatliebe*, fear of "foreign infiltration," and Islamophobia. I describe this kind of wide-ranging recourse to political empathy as a *rhetoric of affection*.

I don't just find this rhetoric of affection personally and politically questionable. It also seems to me to be a curious strategic focus for leftwing or left-liberal parties. Instead, they might consider expressing their solidarity with people with migration histories living in this country—people who nowadays comprise almost a quarter of the German population, of whom nearly half were eligible to vote in the last election. Are they not a future target voting group? Or one could try to actually practice social politics again instead of appropriating *Heimat* terminology—you know, something like real redistribution of resources and wealth? Otherwise, these kinds of social functions are taken over by new rightwing parties like the National Rally/National Front in France or the Law and Justice Party (PiS) in Poland. The much-lauded monograph *Returning to Reims* by French sociologist Didier Eribon is dedicated to uncovering precisely this process: the National Front's acquisition of previously leftwing and Communist milieus.

The rhetoric of affection also stands in polar opposition to the rhetoric of austerity directed at (im)migrants, Muslims, and refugees. It's time to finally trace out the roots of this affection—demonstrated across the democratic spectrum— for voters of the AfD, as well as the lack of empathy for those threatened by rightwing violence. I'm willing to bet that both originate from the same cloudiness that previously obscured the eyes of investigators who failed for so long to recognize the xenophobic profile of the National Socialist Underground. And so it becomes painfully clear that, in a crisis, one shows solidarity for those with whom one feels most closely connected. And that still seems to be the domestic Far Right and not those fleeing from war or poverty abroad. And this, too, is part of the integration paradigm.

Against this backdrop, it becomes easier to understand how political discourse could shift so effortlessly in the direction of nationalism under the influence of an anti-immigrant party like the AfD. Suddenly, everyone wanted and still wants to be proud of their German *Heimat*, whatever the reason. I would record this new *Heimatliebe* as a complete metapolitical victory for the New Right. And this is the precise moment at which the aforementioned dominance of Germany's self-image over its political reality becomes dangerous. Because increasingly, it's becoming less of a deliberate decision to think or act in a *völkisch*-ethnonationalist manner in Germany. Instead, in light of the current rhetoric of our political environment, it requires a decision *not* to do so.

It's becoming more and more apparent that the discourse about integration is part of the problem—not the solution—for our current situation, because it denies empathy to those who perhaps need it most. But the protection from rightwing violence for nearly a quarter of the German population cannot be a question of political persuasion. It is the *obligation* of democratically elected officials in a pluralist society like this one. And yes, I do think that protection from an existential threat is more important than pandering to the ideological concerns of 12.6 percent of the voting populace.

The rightwing delusion of social cohesion is rooted in the fear of fragmentation, panic, and scaremongering about the disintegration of society. These tactics have led us down dark roads historically. Germany collapsed once due to its fragmentation: during the Weimar Republic. And the political Far Right played no small part in that process. Its consequence was fascism—the only truly German revolution—which strove to establish a radical homogenization of social complexities and contradictions. Those same fantasies of conformity are celebrating their return today. Don't give them an inch.

Empathy for rightwing voters is also careless when one considers this country's political future. I don't believe Germany will win the fight against the New Right without the votes of (im)migrant, postmigrant, Jewish, and Muslim citizens. And this critical—if perhaps unfamiliar—new alliance requires strong narratives, the willingness to accept self-criticism from all sides, and a political vision for a society beyond the current integration paradigm.

And yet, wherever I look, I see only the Theaters of Memory and Integration. If you're lucky, the Carnival of Cultures takes place on a summer weekend in Berlin—where everyone can show off how cool their headscarves look and how well they play their musical instruments. Or you go to the Jewish Culture Days to dream to the plaintive melodies of clarinets from a vanished world. Or listen to a corny, Israeli pop star belting out songs anyone in their right mind would immediately tune out. It's an old and dusty truism, trotted out time and again by leftists in their critique of multiculturalism: The staging of culture and diversity for German mainstream society is a very different animal than the actual recognition of diversity. But instead, every German wants to wear a yarmulke and show off how anti-antisemitic they are. In doing so, they probably fail to realize that this yarmulke also gives credence to the most religious elements of Jewishness. As if Deborah Feldman's Hasidic Satmar community in Williamsburg, New York, were really the dominant expression of Jewish life in this country. It's not.

We're a long way away from the point the Right fears society is already at. And, since I'm writing this book to make their vision of social and cultural homogeneity impossible, I've chosen this title: *De*-Integrate!

8

"NO INTEGRATION": DE-INTEGRATION AND ITS PROGENITORS

IN ORDER TO INTERVENE in the German-Jewish Theater of Memory, it is important first to acknowledge that such interventions can also grow to become part of this Theater. In fact, it is probably all but unavoidable that these interventions, too, will—in the words of Maxim Biller—wind up "used up" [*gebraucht*] ("Der gebrauchte Jude"). Even when we focus on de-integration. Because the very existence of living Jews has become a symbol of German reconciliation. Our lives provide a somber pacification of this German desire. Regardless of what we actually do or say. And because of the intractability of this situation, it can become a particular joy for Jewish people to provide objection and dissent. This might be one possible explanation for the passion with which people like Biller, Henryk M. Broder, or Michel Friedman always seemed to have sought out—and continue to seek out—controversy and debate. Conflicts are one way of convincing oneself that our actions have real implications for the ascription we face in German society. And of course, I'm probably also hoping that my own polemic will help open space outside the Theater of Memory.

A wide range of resistance strategies developed over the decades after the end of the War, and these have been employed by both Jewish and other minoritized groups in order to combat role expectations and exclusion. One such strategy is hip-hop. Hip-hop culture originated as an expression of Black American artists' experiences of discrimination, poverty, and resistance. Hip-hop arrived in Germany in the 1980s through the holy trinity of graffiti art, breakdance, and rap music. Some of the first artists to popularize German-language rap music were Haitian-German rapper Torch, the Italian-German rapper Toni-L, and the Afro-German* rapper Linguist. These three rappers combined forces with two additional artists in my own birth year, 1987, to form the hip-hop group Advanced Chemistry. Their first single, "Fremd im eigenen Land" [A Stranger in My Own Country], was released in 1992, and it represented the artists' program. Among other things, their lyrics drew inspiration from the German-Jewish poet Heinrich Heine. The 2001 song "Adriano" tells the story of

---

* The term Afro-German [*afrodeutsch*] was a popular self-designation of empowerment for Black Germans, particularly in the latter decades of the twentieth century. Although the term is still used frequently today, the term Black German is more common in twenty-first century discourse.

Alberto Adriano, who was murdered by neo-Nazis in Dessau in June 2000. Torch raps:[*]

> Now is the time, here is the place
> Tonight's the night Torchmann speaks with grace
> If I think of Germany in the night
> There's no possibility of sleeping tight:
>
> My brother Adriano killed in blood cold
> Skin black. Blood red. Silence is gold
> Thoughts are the deepest blue. A citizen afraid of his
>   own nation
> A German Winter Tale. A velvet blue
> Even as a child I knew it was true:
> I'm a stranger in my own country.

Rap can be an artistic expression of political resistance. Perhaps not in cases like the groups Freundeskreis and Fettes Brot, or the rapper Kollegah—who evolved quickly from a pinup gangster to an outspoken antisemite. But that's a symptom of pop culture: Environmental activists find themselves

---

[*]   The song alludes both to Heine's 1844 "Nachtgedanken" [Night Thoughts] (with its explicit citation of the lines *"Denke ich an Deutschland in der Nacht / Dann bin ich um den Schlaf gebracht"*) as well as the widely banned 1844 satirical epic poem *Deutschland. Ein Wintermärchen* [Germany: A Winter's Tale].

keeping company with conspiracy theorists, klezmer kitsch is displayed alongside a highly reflected New Klezmer movement. Songs of protest and German *Schlager* music. Political bossa nova right next to cringy drum circles at Berlin's Carnival of Cultures. I can only shudder with horror when I remember seeing a former music teacher of mine parade past me at this festival in body paint and a hula skirt.

When I talk about rap music as a form of political resistance in Germany, I'm thinking of bands like Kreuzberg's Thirty-Sixers, who were not only among the first ambassadors of German hip-hop culture, but also actively took up the fight against skinheads and neo-Nazis on the streets of 1980s Kreuzberg (Utlu, "Ins Herz"). They themselves were inspired by the trailblazing German hip-hop artist Maxim, who grew up as Attila Murat Aydın near a US military installation in Berlin-Lichterfelde. Black American soldiers introduced a young Atilla to hip-hop culture there. In the years that followed, Maxim became an evangelist for the new youth culture that was developing in the (im)migrant-influenced, working-class districts of Berlin. He was stabbed to death by a German pensioner on his birthday in 2003 (Kögel, "Geb. 1970"). ז״ל.

Both the Thirty-Sixers and Advanced Chemistry represented clear testaments that those who faced marginalization in German society would no longer permit themselves to be relegated to the peripheries. The vast majority of such interventions have been lost to time, or—as in the case of

Kreuzberg's hip-hop culture—can only be painstakingly reconstructed. Like icebergs, only the outermost extremities of many present-day subcultures receive any media attention, while the broader currents of these movements transpire underground. Such hidden forms of artistic expression provided a treasure trove of resources for my collaboration with author Sasha Marianna Salzmann when we organized the event "Desintegration. Ein Kongress zeitgenössischer jüdischer Positionen" [De-Integration: A Congress of Contemporary Jewish Positionalities] in May 2016 at the Maxim Gorki Theater's Studio Я. Among other things, our De-Integration Congress aimed at combating the common (mis)conception that we and many other contemporary Jewish voices wanted nothing more than to appease German desires. A few lines from the Munich rapper Edgar Wasser—*circa* 2010—seem prescient:

> Am I going too far when I say these things?
> Or do you just need another German flag?
> I can't follow—give me the news!
> Yeah, national pride is trending
>
> I've never seen the like:
> "We've gotten back our pride"—Shut the fuck up!
> This "liberation" of suppressed feelings
> They were suppressed for good reason!

Reprocessing? This doesn't go away
When you smear your face red-black-and-gold!
It's just makeup, yeah, yeah, it's all good fun
I'd rather you just admit how mad you are I'm
    allowed to speak at all . . .

A defining feature of Edgar Wasser's lyrics is the way in which they toy with moral ambivalence. Wasser addresses the normalization of German national pride, revealing the gibberish beneath this whole "We're finally allowed to do this again!" for what it is: "This 'liberation' of suppressed feelings / They were suppressed for good reason!" Like Edgar Wasser, I understand art as a mediated battlefield for political confrontation—as an alternative to Germany's ongoing re-nationalization: "I'd rather you just admit how mad you are I'm allowed to speak at all." I like this definition. It reminds me of when Klezmer musician Daniel Kahn burned an original copy of Hitler's *Mein Kampf* in the courtyard of the Maxim Gorki Theater during the De-Integration Congress for his contribution to the debate around the 2016 republication of this book in Germany for the first time since World War II.

According to a sort of social law of energy conservation, racism and antiracism are always formulated in referential opposition to one another. Both respond to respective interventions from the other side in order to remain up-to-date by constantly redefining themselves. Although they are no longer active today, the project and organization Kanak Attak can also be situated within this larger dynamic. Founded about a decade after the hip-hop groups Advanced Chemistry and the Thirty-Sixers, Kanak Attak was a collaboration between various artists and activists who intervened in the debates of the late 1990s—particularly around the concept of a "multicultural society." Kanak Attak employed elements of exaggeration, hyperbole, and appropriation in their work. For example, they referred to Germany with the Turkish word "Almanya" and replaced the German political talking point of *Multikulturalismus* [multiculturalism] with the Turkish *Mültikültüralizm*. Even the group's name, Kanak Attak,* represented a paradigm shift in the agency and positionality of the minoritized speaker. If the positionality of the (im)migrant or foreign agent had—in public discourse—previously revolved largely around the powerlessness of those subjected to racism, the group now planned its counterstrike: an attempt to wrest back control over defining one's own positionality. Kanak Attak formulated its goal as follows: "to combat the

---

* *Kanak* or *Kanake*—originally derived from the Polynesian word for person—has a long history as a racist term for indigenous people or People of Color in the context of European colonialism. In a German-language context, it is typically employed as a racial slur against people of perceived Mediterranean, North African, or Middle Eastern heritage—though it has more recently been reappropriated within certain postmigrant communities as an expression of self-empowerment.

kanakization of particular groups of people through racist ascription along with its every legal, social, and political consequence" ("Kanak Attak und Basta!"). At the same time, the collective was well aware of the way in which it was becoming established within the larger Theater of Integration. It warned against the appropriation of "Kanakian" cultural products in the German mainstream—a development that had also occurred within US hip-hop culture as it evolved in the 1990s to become one of the most successful, global pop-cultural exports. Just like reggae. And jazz. And, and, and. In 1999, Imran Ayata, one of the cofounders of Kanak Attak, describes this problem in the pop culture magazine *SPEX*:

> Particularly in Berlin, in the context of the current Kanak hype there are a lot of boys and girls who want to participate in the product line for the "boutique of difference." Just look at all the media portraits of Turkish trans people, queers, or female DJs in the Kreuzberg scene. Or they seek out young men who speak Kanak and look just how bourgeois society expects them to. Urban life in the big city likes to appreciate Kanak lifestyle as a kind of "difference chic" just as long as it doesn't actually disrupt the status quo.

And not much has changed in this dynamic over the past twenty years. The rapper Haftbefehl from Offenbach is celebrated in the papers and *Babo* [shot caller] was deemed "teen slang word of the year" in 2013. It almost seems like the whole concept of art as a form of resistance inevitably reverts to self-contradiction: Either you remain out of the orbit of the public eye—remain truly *underground*—and no one recognizes your artistic work, or you are "discovered" and your discovery invites all manner of the same presuppositions and ascriptions you originally opposed. But is there really no alternative to this binary of "invisible or sellout"?

In the same article for *SPEX* magazine, Imran Ayata also comments on the political consequences of interacting with the Theater of Integration:

> Real political issues like equality, structural unemployment, autonomous zones, deportation, and everyday racism disappear under the shadow of public enthusiasm for hybrid, emergent subjects and Kanak performances. But when these social relations aren't thematized, the representative efforts of (im)migrants also ring hollow.

Kanak Attak decided, then, to codetermine the interpretation of their own artistic and cultural expressions. Shortly after the start of the new millennium, their network confronted the German public with the slogan "No Integration!" With this, activists rejected the expectation that they would be willing to integrate into mainstream German society. But the slogan also served as a battle cry against German dominant culture, with its cultivation of the kind of fantasy of an ethnically and culturally harmonious (and homogeneous) society that calls for integration demand.

There are various ways in which such attempts at artistic self-determination are defused. One method is the devaluation of art through categorization: Hip-hop is simply the expression of adolescent street culture. Poetry is apolitical, and so benign. In both cases, this reductionism in the public expectation of the art form results in the exclusion of particular artworks or particular dimensions of this art. Obviously there are other forms of hip-hop than the hypermasculine, battle raps of a Jewish rapper like SpongeBOZZ—although I must say that I enjoyed the video to his song "Yellow Bar Mitzvah." And, of course, there is contemporary, political poetry. I'd be happy to make you some recommendations.

Although the selective evaluation of artistic work may sometimes be necessary, it also simultaneously (and not coincidentally) results in a process of systemic exclusion for those same groups who experience marginalization on a societal level. This has already largely been recognized with regards to the underrepresentation of women throughout the public sphere. But perhaps we should also discuss things like Jewish quotas or a quota for low-income workers or a quota for (im)migrants at institutions of higher education. I'm not joking. But exclusion is not merely engendered by committees and institutions; forms of categorizing art also serve to divide up artistic productions into tiny drawers and boxes labeled with unostentatious adjectives. Words—in a German context—like "migrant," "Muslim," "feminist," or "Jewish." These adjectives serve as labels through which potential audiences or readers come to expect "authentic," biographical works—and, at the same time, works of art that do not meet the criteria of German "high culture," which follows its own set of rules and expresses an inimitability of culture that can only be achieved by those Peter Handkes and Sibylle Lewitscharoffs of the German-speaking world.

Particularly in the context of this "adjective literature," the same forms of exclusion are perpetuated that feminist, Jewish, migrant, postmigrant, or Black literature sought to thematize and problematize in the first place by highlighting the particularities of their own perspectives. What a depressing outcome. After all, visibility and the demarcation of their own respective positionalities were—originally—central strategies of such movements in seeking to anticipate and preempt cultural appropriation. You can observe this same phenomenon in the discourse of authenticity in the world of theater. Or in the way that Jewish art in Germany seems limited to three topics: antisemitism, the Shoah, and Israel. If you think it's going too far to say we dug our own graves by always falling into these same traps, at the very least we should agree that we've provided our own shovels.

But artistic self-empowerment and artistic critiques are also rendered invisible by a specific kind of cultural appropriation. A case study of this phenomenon can be found in the interpretation of the poetry of Paul Celan: Celan was and often still is described as a hermetic or radically subjective poet whose perspectives are incredibly difficult to understand from the outside. And it could very well be that these interpretations of his poetry contributed to his ascent to canonization on the Mount Olympus of German literature. But this alleged hermetic seal certainly did not prevent classroom discussion of "Todesfuge" (which, contrary to a hermetic interpretation, has actually proven to have very concrete dimensions). Quite the contrary: This apparent simultaneity provides a critical prerequisite for the very kind of appropriation I mean. The specificity of interpretation provides for a limited range of discussion—it renders only excerpts visible. Celan's direct association with the horrors of the Holocaust can be contrasted with his alleged "hermeticism" in order to ignore the unsettling anger and revenge his passages might otherwise suggest. This line of interpretation therefore helps domesticate the danger which Jewish art could otherwise pose for the German positionality. From Celan to hip-hop, the artistic expressions of marginalized positionalities are defanged for integration into the cultural mainstream.

Kanak Attak attempted to position itself against this kind of appropriation and trivializing. From the mid-1980s on, the

Afro-German movement manifested parallel developments which can, for example, be observed in both the poetic and scholarly works of Ghanaian-German activist May Ayim (May Opitz). From the early 2000s on, the influence of studies on Critical Whiteness from the United States provided further impulses, and resulted in works such as *Deutschland Schwarz Weiß* [Germany Black and White] by author and musician Noah Sow, or *Plantation Memories* by artist and psychologist Grada Kilomba. To be sure, the designation of the dominant social perspective as "white gaze" that was common at that time provided an important impulse for my own designation of what I describe in this book as the "German positionality" or simply as "German" vis-à-vis other minoritized positions. The 2010 *Kara Günlük. Die geheimen Tagebücher des Sesperado* [Kara Günlük: The Secret Diary of the Sesperado] by Berlin author and activist Mutlu Ergün-Hamaz also deserves mention. Ergün-Hamaz manages to synthesize a connection between critiques of the functionalization of Kanak cultures and critiques of structural racism through the concept of Critical Whiteness.

These aforementioned works by artists and activists contributed significantly to the way in which marginalized, minoritized groups came to conceptualize empowerment and self-determination in sociopolitical debates. I remain convinced that theater, hip-hop culture, and literature today continue to maintain the greatest potential both for critiquing, but also for overcoming the Theaters of Memory and Integration. Just think back on any of the more significant sociopolitical scandals of the past decade—incidents that inspired days or even weeks or months of discussion across print, digital, and social media: Again and again, the arts took on the role of holding up a funhouse mirror to dominant culture: allowing it to be subverted, questioned, queered. Revealing its ugliness or ignorance. Just think of the "avenidas" debates of 2017, the debates around blackface in 2012, the Böhmermann affair in 2016, or the 2018 Echo Music Prize awarded to rappers Kollegah and Farid Bang and their antisemitic provocations . . . * The next scandal is

---

*   The controversy around the poem "avenidas" by Eugen Gomringer is discussed briefly in Chapter 5. In 2012, the use of blackfacing at the Deutsches Theater for a staging of the play *Unschuld* [Innocence] by Dea Loher inspired widespread public protest and new conversations about the prevalence of racist practices in German theater culture. The so-called Böhmermann affair (or Erdogate) was a scandal involving German comedian Jan Böhmermann's repeated insults to the controversial Turkish president Recep Tayyip Erdoğan—an offense (insulting a foreign head of state) that, at the time, remained punishable by law according to archaic German legal code. The corresponding international incident resulted in the comedian's pending (and eventually dropped) prosecution, as well as an amendment to modernize the existing law. The Echo Music Prize was a long-running staple of the German music industry. In the final year of the award's presentation, the prize for Best Hip-Hop/Urban Album of the year was awarded to Kollegah and Farid Bang, whose album contained an off-color joke comparing their own muscle definition to that of starving Jews in Auschwitz's death camps. Their nomination, as well as the decision to allow them to perform the track at the award ceremony, inspired widespread protest.

bound to come, and you can be sure that art will continue to play a leading role.

In this context, I understand de-integration as a Jewish contribution to the larger postmigrant project, the goal of which is to understand and advance radical diversity as the very foundation of German society. When we consider the Jewish angle on the concept of de-integration, it's important to focus on the history of Jewish self-empowerment in post-National Socialist Germany, as well. This reflection should start with the Jewish survivors and those who returned to the German-speaking world after 1945. I have dedicated an entire chapter to them. For now, I would like to turn, instead, to the infamous Fassbinder controversy that I understand as a sort of Jewish Kanak Attak.

In order to better understand this, dear readers, I would like to ask you to kindly remind yourselves that there was no real organized Jewish resistance to the German Theater of Memory in the first decades after the War. One could argue that it took until the 1970s for West Germany's Jewish population's own self-confidence to develop to such a degree that they were finally able to offer something like a public opposition to Germany's self-conception at that time. Their opportunity came during a discussion of a work by Rainer Werner Fassbinder. Born in 1945, the author and filmmaker was considered something of an enfant terrible in the cultural landscape of 1970s West Germany. In the 1974–1975 season, he served as co-artistic director at the Theater am Turm in Frankfurt am Main, where he also wrote the play *Der Müll, die Stadt und der Tod* [Garbage, the City, and Death]. Based on the novel *Die Erde ist unbewohnbar wie der Mond* [The Earth is as Uninhabitable as the Moon] by 1968-generation author Gerhard Zwerenz, the play thematized—among other things—the construction of Frankfurt's exclusive Westend district.

It was rumored that Ignatz Bubis—then a member of the executive board of the Jewish Community in Frankfurt [Jüdische Gemeinde Frankfurt] and later the aforementioned *sitting* president of the Central Council of Jews in Germany during Martin Walser's fateful speech at St. Paul's Church—had been Fassbinder's model for his figure of the "wealthy Jew." In this figure's utterly exaggerated character profile, the wealthy Jew is described as a Jewish speculator, motivated only by his desire for revenge, his perversion, and his greed. Already in Fassbinder's own lifetime, the work received broad criticism and was only staged within a very limited circle. But a mere ten years later, Fassbinder had died an untimely death, and the new artistic director of the Schauspiel Frankfurt, former *FAZ* feuilleton chief editor Günther Rühle, decided to bring this work to the mainstage. The resulting protest culminated on the day of the premiere on October 31, 1985, with more than a thousand protestors demonstrating before the theater. Just as the curtains were about to part, the stage was occupied by thirty, mostly elderly members of the Jewish Community in Frankfurt.

What a shock! Suddenly living Jewish people had taken the stage demanding their right to political participation while a German audience had only been able to imagine them as bent and emaciated figures from the ghettos of history, Wall Street moneybags, or soldiers from conflicts in the Near East. Oy, I would have loved to have been there, but was born two years too late! While conducting research for this book, I pored over archival documentation of the ensuing debates. There were times when I was greatly amused. And there were times—and this is not particularly surprising—when my laughter caught in my throat. The kind of chutzpah it took from representatives of German dominant culture—from the play's first mention all the way through to their reactions at the occupation of the theater—to tell Jews just what they would have to suffer in a normalized Germany: a sickening display of arrogance. Artistic director Rühle proclaimed "closed season is over" [*Ende der Schonzeit*]—which, fittingly enough, was also the subtitle of a collection of these debates compiled by Heiner Lichtenstein the following year. And what else could Rühle have meant by this obscene expression, Henryk M. Broder writes in his period contribution to the *Süddeutsche Zeitung*, except that it was now, once again, open season for hunting Jews in Germany:

If Rühle also postulates a new beginning for the normalization of German-Jewish relations by proclaiming the end of "closed season," and, at the same time, promotes himself by espousing this new normality, then he is simply offering a salon-appropriate version of the same demand already long-postulated by the *Nationalzeitung*: This cannot go on any longer; a line must finally be drawn in the sand. ("Antisemitismus").

It should not go unmentioned that Rühle filed a defamation suit against Broder for his assessment of the "closed season is over" scandal. The legal case ended a year later with the settlement that Rühle had only spoken of "closed season" in the sense of a "conservation area" (Schueler, "Was hat der Frankfurter"). Rühle's words provide a brutal illustration of what a German desire for normalization can also lead to— and they were in accordance with the views of many other leading intellectuals of the day. The old boys sat around their regulars' table at the local pub, slammed their tankards down on the greasy tabletop and proclaimed: "Well, we had to do it eventually!"

Meanwhile, Jewish people in Frankfurt did what so many other Jewish people in this country should have been doing: They declined to play along with this version of normalization. Which is why I've dubbed their intervention a Jewish Kanak Attak. The parameters of their actions contributed to a new and uniquely Jewish discourse—one that had already been developing for decades, since the end of the War, but had yet to receive attention in the public sphere. This sense of autonomy also became visible in period debates that extended beyond the opposition of opponents and advocates of the play itself, and quickly developed into the opposition of German and Jewish positionalities (though one must, of course, acknowledge a number of German allies who supported these Jewish positionalities). But you've probably never heard about these events at all. Just like you didn't follow our recess conversations fifteen years later on the playgrounds of Jewish schools, the contents of our seminars supported by the Ernst Ludwig Ehrlich Scholarship Fund, or our late-night meetings in Jewish cemeteries. We're part of banking and the media, supermarkets and the ensembles of German theaters again.

We're back.

9

LIKE THEY DO IN BABYLON:
ON JEWISH DIVERSITY

IT'S TYPICAL to speak of the "Jewish community" in Germany as though it were something self-evident, homogeneous, and easily defined. I'm pretty happy that I've largely been able to avoid using this term so far (except in those cases where it is part of an official title, or where I have already begun to problematize it as a concept). Of course, Jewish people don't necessarily comprise any kind of community whatsoever—neither religious nor ethnic. Germany's living Jewish population today hasn't been this diverse since well before the Second World War. And so this chapter is dedicated to the potential of our disunity—because our lack of uniformity is not simply an inconvenience: It might represent a key resource for Jewish de-integration. The primary source of our current differences can be traced back to the many waves of Jewish immigration (mainly) since the early 1990s. Between 1991 and 2004, more than 200,000 people of Jewish heritage immigrated to Germany from the former Soviet Union as "quota refugees." These people (and their descendants) comprise 90 percent of the approximately 100,000 official members of Jewish congregations in Germany today. But just as many of these immigrants chose not to become members of any established Jewish congregation. In the 1990s, I went to school with the children of these recent immigrants at the newly founded Jüdische Schule Berlin [Jewish School of Berlin], which is today known as the Jüdisches Gymnasium Moses Mendelssohn [Moses Mendelssohn Jewish Secondary School]. It was the first Jewish school to be established in Germany since National Socialism.

Edited by Dmitrij Belkin and Raphael Gross, the 2010 collection *Ausgerechnet Deutschland!* [Germany, of All Places!] provides a far-ranging survey of Germany's post-Soviet community, and it also served as the source for my own statistics on Jewish immigration. As they've grown up, the children of these Jewish immigrants have taken on increasingly important roles in the German public sphere—figures like authors Sasha Marianna Salzmann, Lena Gorelik, Olga Grjasnowa, or Dmitrij Kapitelman. They've come to represent an unexpected answer to the questions about integrating these recent (im)migrants that arose in various Jewish communities during the 1990s: Because those who have today come to co-determine the discourse about Jewish people in Germany by and large did *not* choose to become members of official Jewish congregations. They have, instead, created new spaces of their own.

A second group of Jewish immigrants began arriving—predominantly in Berlin—from Israel after the turn of the millennium. Because many of these immigrants were far more radical than their post-Soviet predecessors, they often found little welcome in the rigid structures of Berlin's Jewish community. They took action accordingly by establishing their own comfortable, Jewish parallel societies as an alternative to German "organized Jewry," as Doron Kiesel, scientific director for the Education Department of the Central Council of Jews in Germany, once jokingly described it. Actually, I find his description entirely accurate. Israelis represented a critical addition to Berlin's Jewish life, its food, as well as its party scene. Their sense of independence was surely influenced in no small part by the fact that they'd grown up in the only predominantly Jewish society on earth. This also permits Israeli-German artists such as playwright Sivan Ben Yishai, painter Ofri Lapid, or composer Amir Shpilman to define their own positionalities in Germany with a distinctly stable sense of Jewish identity. Which is something extraordinary for the vast majority of Jewish people who grew up in Germany.

Since the 1990s, West German Jewish communities have also been influenced by a notably smaller group of Jewish people from the former East Germany. This includes people like the aforementioned Mirna Funk and Anetta Kahane, publicist and activist Stella Leder, or my own aunt, Leah Carola Czollek—founder of the Institute for Social Justice and Diversity, which has contributed to the development of queer positionalities both inside and beyond Reform Jewish communities (Lohaus, Knödler, Yun, "Bist du . . . "). Not to mention the author of the extraordinary book you're currently holding in your hands. Jewish people from the German Democratic Republic brought something of the leftist Jewish tradition back to Jewish debates in Germany—something very fundamental to my own critique of Jewish self-presentation in the German present day.

The arrival of these three groups in a newly Reunified Germany shifted the center of Jewish life in Germany distinctly in the direction of Berlin, away from its previous seat in Frankfurt am Main. And this shift helped reestablish a small part of the prewar situation for Jewish life in Germany— albeit with markedly different portents. The new demographic situation came to be supported by the establishment of new Jewish institutions: alongside the increasing number of Jewish preschools, kindergartens, and schools, the Ernst Ludwig Ehrlich Scholarship Fund was established in 2008 to support promising Jewish university students. It functions as a kind of think tank, developing new perspectives on the Jewish present in Germany. A number of Jewish organizations have also become active at German universities, including Hillel, Studentim, and the European Union of Jewish Students. For the first time since 1933, Jewish youth in Germany can attend Jewish institutions for the course of their entire education.

The intensifying quest for a Jewish role beyond the confines of German dominant cultural ascriptions might well be a result of the growing availability of these spaces for Jewish reflection.

I have already argued that today's critique of the Theater of Memory would have been unthinkable in the first decades after the defeat of National Socialism. In the 1950s, after the US occupiers incrementally began to withdraw from their direct involvement in German politics, Jewish people in West Germany were left with few other options than to orient themselves according to mainstream German society. At the same time, following the Slánský trial in Prague in 1952 and its East German equivalent with the arrest of Paul Merker, a wave of antisemitic persecution swept out of the Soviet Union. This resulted in the flight of the leadership of East Germany's Jewish communities, along with hundreds of its Jewish citizens, who escaped to West Germany in January 1953. The Jewish populations of both East and West Germany were left with little choice other than to conform to the demands of state power—or flee their countries.

The limited options available to Jewish people in the post-war Germanies was not merely due to increasing German autonomy or the relatively small number of survivors; it was—as I have already hinted—also impacted by an exclusion from global Jewish communities. Jewish life in Germany after the Shoah was widely considered illegitimate and morally reprehensible, and so Jewish people living in Germany were largely ignored by international Jewish institutions. Michal Bodemann observes:

> From about 1949 on, Jewish people in West Germany lost their connections, and with them, their status: The Allies viewed the new Federal Republic of Germany as an important partner, and so they transitioned away from their own self-definition as an anti-Nazi occupying force in Germany. From a Jewish perspective, they switched camps from the Jewish to the German side. Jewish aid groups began to diminish as the bulk of the Jewish population migrated to Israel or North America [. . .] Those who remained in West Germany suddenly found themselves isolated: pariahs in the Jewish world because they had remained in Germany, and a diminished minority at home—impoverished, traumatized, and largely unloved or even hated. It was out of this situation—and not immediately in 1945, as the official Jewish narrative likes to portray it—that the new Jewish community came to define itself as we know it today. The new Jewish leadership in Germany [. . .] made the opportunistic decision of running to their German counterparts with open arms. ("Endzeit," 9)

There are Jewish voices today, as well, who remain critical of or outright reject the obvious attraction of Berlin for Jewish people worldwide. One example of this can be found in the

2014 conflict around the migration of Israeli Jews to Berlin that became known as the "Milky Protest." Milky is an Israeli pudding brand. At the time, a Facebook page called Olim L'Berlin had begun evaluating the differences between Berlin and Tel Aviv—including a survey of the price of Milky's chocolate pudding. The site recommended immigrating to Berlin, in part due to the low cost of chocolate pudding there. The word "Olim" is otherwise used exclusively to refer to immigration to Israel. The chocolate pudding posts ignited a debate that eventually even came to involve prominent Israeli politicians. While some used the opportunity to thematize the high cost of groceries in Israel at large, others went so far as to decry the fact that the Zionist project could be abandoned for something as petty as cheap pudding. That *Germany* of all places was the intended destination for these Israeli emigrants probably didn't help.

Of course, the current situation is fundamentally different from that of the *Sh'erit ha-Pletah*—the surviving remnants, as Jewish survivors after the Shoah came to understand themselves in Germany. The first decades were largely consumed by the Jewish population's own story of survival and their justification for remaining in the land of the perpetrators. Jewish people in Germany at that time were isolated, and many had a guilty conscience for not immigrating to Israel or the USA as so many others had. And so it was understandable that they became fixated on their own presence in the country of the perpetrators. A constant, mantric repetition in literature, speeches, and films contributed to the way in which images of packed or unpacked suitcases, candles, fiddles, and the general black-and-white aesthetic became established as the eternal clichés of Jewish art even before the boom that followed in the wake of the student movements of 1968.

The public demand for "the Jew" was not always as high as it was during the time in which I, myself, became a Jew for Germans. And from a Jewish perspective, people were still excited about all this newfound attention in the 1980s: the increased visibility of Jewish literature, Jewish cultural days, and Jewish music. I respect this sense of relief, and I don't want my concept of de-integration to make light of the situations and the difficulties that previous generations faced in any way. De-integration would not have been the right strategy for those times—just as I hope, in twenty years, that we will be in a different situation than we are today. But for the time being, the (im)migration of Jewish people from the former Soviet Union and Israel has created new possibilities for self-definition that we must pursue.

However, possibilities are not the same thing as realities. Examples like the presentation of the Berlin Maccabiah Games as a Jewish "summer's tale" illustrate how strongly the present behavior of Jewish people continues to conform to predesignated boundaries and prescribed forms of representation. There are two connected reasons for this phenomenon:

The first is the German demand for the association of Jews with the Holocaust—a basic component part of the German Theater of Memory. The second is the central role of the Shoah in *Jewish* self-definition in this country. The connection between these two aspects can be illustrated with the 2006 opening of the Ohel Jakob Synagogue in Munich. In order to reach the main sanctuary—and, you know, pray and utilize the building for its religious function—it is first necessary to walk through an underground passageway on whose walls are inscribed the names of concentration camps and the dead. I honestly find this a bit intrusive. It's problematic that Jews are *compelled* to connect religious practice with the Shoah in this way. The Shoah has nothing to do with my religion.

Hopes that the Theater of Memory might already have been rendered obsolete after the first waves of Jewish (im)migrants from the former Soviet Union proved to be premature. In the 2010 collection *Ausgerechnet Deutschland!*, Sergey Lagodinsky writes:

> Germans awoke from the guilty slumber of a nation of Sleeping Beauties. Their newfound sense of German national identity no longer requires Jews for its self-assurance. It cries out for a normality grounded in the successful navigation of the World Cup and not in special greetings for the functionaries of Jewish organizations on the International Day of

Holocaust Remembrance. [...] After decades of therapeutic occupation with its own history, today's Germany is more preoccupied with itself: its here and now. (168)

I would like to add that this German preoccupation with the present does not, in any way, mean that Germany has closed the doors on continuities with its Nazi past. In the aforementioned 2018 survey conducted by Andreas Zick and Jonas Rees, the majority of participants answered that the Fall of the Berlin Wall was more important for their own identities than either the Holocaust or World War II. And I'm not sure that this is factually true. What these participants are expressing here instead, I think, is their own *desire* for a reality in which Reunification plays a greater role than Germany's crimes. So I'd rather think about the extent to which Germany's relationship to its Jews has shifted over the past years. Because in their newfound identification with the victims of National Socialism, the Germans suffer alongside the Jews. *Our* mothers, *our* fathers.

But I fully agree with Lagodinsky's analysis that every pause in the Theater of Memory must be utilized toward developing an autonomous Jewish self-conception. Our goal should be to formulate new, alternative narratives to the never-ending story of the Theater of Memory. In his conclusion, Michal Bodemann writes:

Only the Germans can process their own history. The Jews need play no role—neither in glorifying nor in overcoming the German past. And so it follows that Jewish people in Germany must make great efforts to look inward and allow it to grow quiet around them. For the sake of their own salvation, they must not allow themselves to be tempted and seduced by the co-optation or instrumentalization of their environment—however this may transpire. They must, instead, reinforce their own shared structures: socially, culturally, and pluralistically. (*Gedächtnistheater*, 178–79)

For the time being, we can't expect this kind of self-reflection on our own role in the Theater of Memory to come from organizations like the Central Council of Jews in Germany. In 2014, one of its events on the topic of "Memory and Trauma in the Third Generation" bore the title: "A Never Ending Story." There was no question mark. And yet, important impulses for critiquing the alleged correspondence between the Jewish self-image in Germany and the Jewish role in the German Theater of Memory can be located in the post-Soviet and Israeli (im) migrant communities. For example, the idea has already gained traction here in Germany that Jewish people from the former Soviet Union and their descendants celebrate May 9th as Victory Day Over Fascism. Completely independent of the ideological significance of this date during Communist times (or still in Russia, today), memories of victory over Nazi

Germany represent a radical break from November 9th and January 27th,[*] which are the central dates for the German remembrance of the murder of European Jews. The narrative of (post-)Soviet Jewish people is not one of liberation from the death camps of Auschwitz, but rather one of having liberated these camps. And this represents a very significant difference, indeed. The following scene plays out in my mind's eye: at the next remembrance event, I see the familiar sight of two rows of standing figures: the Germans on one side, the Jews on the other. But instead of a staging of the standard ritual between the contrite (but rehabilitated) Germans and their sorrowful victims, this time an enactment of the Jewish liberators and the defeated Germans unfolds. One of the Jews bends down to a prone German, pats him on the head, and whispers: Don't worry, after all, we won the War!

Of course, the reality is quite different. In interviews, it's standard for me—regardless of the context of the interview itself—to be asked questions about my own experiences with antisemitism. Or about my family history. In the end, it's always obvious that they really want to hear something about the Shoah. If I decline, or if I simply have nothing fitting to

---

[*] The anniversary of *Pogromnacht* (also referred to as *Kristallnacht* [The Night of Broken Glass]) and the International Day of Holocaust Remembrance on the anniversary of the liberation of Auschwitz, respectively. See Chapter 10 for a more in-depth discussion.

say on the matter, I can see the obvious disappointment in the eyes of my interviewer. When one thinks of Jewish people in this country, images of long-bearded shtetl inhabitants come to mind—wig-wearing Yiddish *mamen*, neurotic salon owners, Haskalah Mendelssohns, or the kindly grandchildren of Holocaust survivors. One never thinks of Jewish People of Color, which excludes a vast range of Jewish experiences from potential representation, a range stretching from the Mizrahi of North Africa to Afghanistan and the Beta Israel of Ethiopia.

The Jewish community is far more diverse than the public utility of Jews in Germany would suggest. And this diversity has time and again been an important reason for me to reflect on my own Jewish positionality. I am reminded of my encounter with the works of Israeli poet Adi Keissar, a few of whose poems I had the honor of translating into German. Keissar's parents are from Yemen, and are—along with Jewish people from other places like Iran, Iraq, or Morocco—Mizrahi Jews. In Israel, where most cultural standards are oriented around the culture of Ashkenazi Jews who emigrated from Europe and the United States, Mizrahi identity is often associated with being unclean, working class, loud, or uncouth. This encounter with Adi Keissar had a profound impact on my own understanding of Jewish identity. Firstly, because I found it nearly impossible to reproduce the complexity of internal Jewish power dynamics within the available coordinate field of Jewish representation in Germany. And secondly, because through my work with Adi Keissar's poetry, I came to recognize the great extent to which my own understanding of Jewish identity had been oriented around Ashkenazi perspectives.

And this was truly a critical insight for me. Adi Keissar had denounced her own integration into Ashkenazi-Israeli dominant culture in 2001 with the founding of the poetry-reading series "Ars Poetica." In an Israeli context, this title not only references the "art of poetry" in the tradition of the Roman poet Horace, it also recalls the pejorative Hebrew word *arsim* [pimp], which is commonly used as a racial slur against Jewish people of Mizrahi descent. Ars Poetica is open to anyone—but its combination of poetry and party, belly dancing and spoken word, makes a clear counterclaim to Ashkenazi cultural hegemony. The tremendous success of this bold new reading format renders the idea of a traditional podium reading—a reception with a glass of wine and chamber music—as simply one of many legitimate possibilities. And this, in turn, puts pressure on the monopoly of Ashkenazi poetic representation as the expression of Israeli high culture.

Adi Keissar's works also allowed me to understand the possibility of creating Jewish art without a biographical connection to the Shoah: the ways in which this alters thematic and formal priorities. In a German context, an analysis of internal Jewish differences could thus lay the groundwork for de-integration. And since becoming cognizant of the diversity of Jewish experience, I find myself increasingly aware of the number of Jewish people I encounter whose family histories transcend the (hi)story of German crimes—whose (hi)stories might intersect with these events, but continue in every conceivable direction. A former classmate of mine whose parents came from Morocco and Turkey, a friend in Brussels with a German father and a Tunisian mother, a journalist from a Jewish periodical with a mother from Iran . . . It's almost like it wasn't until I, myself, became conscious of internal Jewish diversity that I developed the ears to listen to its many voices—and more importantly, to value them as further facets of Jewishness.

But of course, I'm writing this book because I have a problem. My problem is that my own conception of Jewishness began with an enormous pile of corpses. And for a long time, I was unable to think or write beyond this macabre mountain. Walter Benjamin's famous description of Paul Klee's monoprint *Angelus Novus* was easy for me to visualize: his back turned toward the future, his wings caught by the storm blowing from Paradise. The angel is no longer able to close his wings, no longer able to turn and face the future. Benjamin describes the angel as seeing only one single catastrophe: the pile of wreckage and debris we call history. In my version, the angel could no longer see anything but the history of its *own* destruction.

My work with Adi Keissar's poetry also made me aware of my own complacency with German trauma and the German imaginary of Jews as victims of their own historic crimes.

Now, I don't want to give the impression that this initial encounter allowed me simply to overcome my own complacency. Because I don't believe the goal of de-integration can be a *complete* escape from one's own entanglements with the Theater of Memory. That seems like part of an unrealistic and ultimately detrimental fantasy of absolute consistency. To live in Germany as a Jewish person also means experiencing and sharing in the influence of German history and the depths of its many precipices. I face problems here that I wouldn't face in other places, but these are my problems and I wouldn't trade them with anyone. Not even with Adi Keissar. Because de-integration also means recognizing the depths of one's own precipices. Which leads to a rejection of the role of the Good Victim. The promise of de-integration is not redemption, but a greater degree of self-determination.

Further analysis of Germany's increasing Jewish diversity offers the chance for critical reflection on internal Jewish positionalities and power relations. But because this kind of self-critique is—inevitably—also a challenge to the role ascription of the Theater of Memory, it also offers a critique of German-Jewish relations. Jewish people come from different places; they have different sexual preferences, and different religious and political practices. If we are able to take these differences seriously—by which I mean: make a serious effort to recognize their validity and incorporate this into our own vision of Jewish identity—this represents a step in the right direction. Movement toward a new sense of German, European, international Jewishness.

But, of course, the decision to distance oneself from the Theater of Memory also includes potential risks like the loss of the important social and material recognition that German dominant culture provides when we accept our Jewish roles. Fear of this loss may help explain the fact that even many critical Jewish voices continue to accept the expectations and ascriptions of the German public. Creating an alternative to the Theater of Memory also means fashioning one's own alternative spaces for recognition and for forging new alliances. And there is good reason to do so—not least the fact that not every Jewish person was once liberated from Auschwitz. Jewish life in Germany is Ashkenazi and furious, Mizrahi and queer, impoverished and Reform, narrow-minded and excessive, clean-shaven and Orthodox. And perhaps we are only just now learning how to recognize our own diversity. Doing this justice means forsaking the Theater of Memory.

Jewish life in Germany today presents us with a better basis upon which to create new spaces and develop something like an autonomous Jewish identity than at any other time since the Second World War. Some of us have already gotten started.

10

INGLOURIOUS POETS: REVENGE AS SELF-EMPOWERMENT

WHO EXACTLY WAS IT that decided figures like Shakespeare's Shylock from *The Merchant of Venice* or Fassbinder's wealthy Jew in *Der Müll, die Stadt und der Tod* were antisemitic projections? Why do we not, instead, turn the tables, change perspectives, and reread these same texts? What exactly is it that Shylock says in *The Merchant of Venice*? Those famous words that everyone who knows anything about this play can probably (at least partially) recite:

> Hath not a Jew eyes? Hath not a Jew hands, organs, dimensions, senses, affections, passions? Fed with the same food, hurt with the same weapons, subject to the same diseases, healed by the same means, warmed and cooled by the same winter and summer, as a Christian is? If you prick us, do we not bleed? If you tickle us, do we not laugh? If you poison us, do we not die? And if you wrong us, shall we not revenge?

If we are like you in the rest, we will resemble you in that. If a Jew wrong a Christian, what is his humility? Revenge. If a Christian wrong a Jew, what should his sufferance be by Christian example? Why, revenge. The villainy you teach me, I will execute, and it shall go hard but I will better the instruction. (97–99)

It's obvious why the figure of Shylock can also function as a honeytrap for antisemitic interpretation. Shylock's monologue contains all the same fearful projections of the vengeful, greedy Jew. But let's be honest here: Place your hand over your heart. Is it not *also* perfectly conceivable after the pogroms, after two thousand years of discrimination at the hands of Christian overlords, and after a particularly fucked-up twentieth century—would it even be the least bit surprising—that a timeless Jewish desire for revenge might also have developed? Regardless of the antisemitic clichés, is the desire for revenge on the part of the Jewish characters not also perfectly, politically plausible? "And if you wrong us, shall we not revenge?" Honestly: "Wrong us" seems like quite a euphemism when you reread these lines in the context of the twentieth century and the attempted murder of *all* European Jews. I mean, doesn't all of that just kind of justify and legitimize a Jewish desire for revenge?

In Chapter 5, I discussed the relief felt by a prominent post-war intellectual after he interpreted "[not] one single word of hatred" in Nelly Sachs' poetry for those "hangmen and everything else that renders us their confidants and accomplices." But his fear of potential Jewish vengeance actually says more about its justification than the author probably intended. And meanwhile, a different tradition of Jewish postwar history—a (hi)story of resistance and revenge—was developing behind the scenes.

Rainer Werner Fassbinder's 1978 film *In einem Jahr mit 13 Monden* [In a Year of 13 Moons] presents a great number of similarities with his aforementioned, scandal-ridden play *Der Müll, die Stadt und der Tod*. Its cast of characters includes a successful Jewish real-estate speculator whose business model reflects the practices he learned from the Germans in their concentration camps. A similar figure appears—under very different circumstances—in Maxim Biller's 1990 short story "Wenn ich einmal reich und tot bin" [Someday When I'm Rich and Dead]. And the commonalities between these characters demonstrate the way in which the actions of an alleged antisemitic figure—the ruthless accumulation of property on the part of a Jewish concentration camp survivor—can also serve as a motif of Jewish revenge. Because the wealthy Jew in Biller's short story may be arrogant and amoral, but his desire for vengeance seems entirely relatable. Just like with Holocaust-related humor, the question of antisemitism vs. self-empowerment is also one of context.

This chapter examines real-life examples of Jewish revenge, followed by an analysis of how the topoi of Jewish vengeance have found artistic representation since the Shoah. Both real-life Jewish vengeance and revenge art offer a subversive contrast to the Theater of Memory by providing a counterfigure to the model of the peaceful, defenseless Jewish victim. In presenting the all-but-forgotten memories of Jewish revenge, such narratives also become an archive of resistance. They create space to reflect upon the ways in which the violence of the Holocaust has been written onto Jewish bodies, Jewish psyches, and Jewish language(s): spaces for mourning. As a legitimate, psychological mechanism for processing this trauma, these narratives also become a form of self-empowerment.

In order to better understand Jewish actions during the Shoah, it is important to differentiate between resistance and revenge. While resistance is always aimed directly against the oppressor, revenge is often postponed or deferred. Resistance can be a form of revenge, but revenge is not resistance. Organized and unorganized forms of resistance occurred in virtually every place where Jewish people were persecuted during the Second World War (Lustiger, *Zum Kampf*). And we only know about uprisings and other activities in the ghettos and concentration camps when survivors lived to tell the tale. Their stories depict courage in the face of desperation, and a tremendous will to make their own annihilation as difficult as possible for the Nazi aggressors. The Warsaw

Ghetto Uprising from April 19 through May 16, 1943, is the most widely known example of such resistance. But resistance also took place in the form of paramilitary activities beyond the ghetto walls. Historians Jim G. Tobias and Peter Zinke estimate that there were approximately 15,000 active Jewish partisans in Lithuania, Poland, and the Western Soviet Union alone (24). The poet Hirsch Glik was one of them. He authored the unofficial partisan anthems "Zog nit keyn mol" [Never Say Never] and "Shtil, di nakht iz oysgeshternt" [Quiet, the Night is Full of Stars]. "Shtil" is narrated from the perspective of a young female resistance fighter, and it tells the story of a successful, but ultimately futile attack on a Nazi convoy. Hirsch Glik was murdered shortly before the end of the War. He was twenty-two years old.

With the end of the War, the register shifted from resistance to revenge. Revenge is not merely a form of reparation and self-empowerment; it is also a form of punishment. One example of this was the Jewish Brigade trained in British-occupied Palestine who fought alongside the Allies on different fronts throughout the second half of the War. Distinguished by a Star of David on their military insignia, nearly five thousand of these Jewish volunteers were stationed in the Italian city of Tarvisio by the end of World War II. Alongside their military roles, the Jewish Brigade were charged with facilitating Jewish survivors' escape to Israel—largely along illegal routes. A smaller subset of the Brigade was also responsible for hunting down and bringing those Nazi officials to justice who had played important roles in the Holocaust and were now hiding out in Austria and northern Italy. If you're interested in this history, I'd recommend the 2013 ORF documentary film *Killing Nazis*.

Around the same time, in Bucharest, a group of former resistance fighters and other survivors had assembled around the poet and Vilnian partisan leader Abba Kovner to plan and orchestrate revenge. Their plans exceeded those of the Jewish Brigade. Kovner's group was known by the acronym DIN (which also means "judgment" in Hebrew). The acronym itself stood for "Dam Yehudi Note" [The Blood of Israel Avenges]. Their program is described in a memoir by a leader of the leftist Zionist organization Dror in Białystok, Zipora Birman, who was murdered in a German concentration camp in occupied Poland. Her text can be understood as something of a party platform for DIN:

> The obligation to seek vengeance has been imposed upon all of you. Not one of you shall find peace, not one of you shall sleep, not one of you shall find rest. And as we have walked in the shadow of death, so shall you live: in the sanctity of vengeance for the blood that has been spilled. May they be accursed who read these lines, sigh, and go about their daily lives; accursed, those who are content to shed their tears, for they forget our souls. We call upon you for vengeance,

vengeance without mercy, without feeling, and without talk of the "Good Germans." The Good Germans shall die an easy death. They shall be the last to die, just as they promised their "Good Jews": a death by gunshot wound. (Tobias & Zinke, 100)

For Zipora Birman, those murdered during the Holocaust will only find their rest through vengeance: a collective revenge that enacts that same, undifferentiated violence upon the Germans that they enacted upon the Jews. Revenge, in this document, takes on a quasi-religious dimension with Old Testament parallels. The biblical tale of Samson ends with a final act of vengeance against the Philistines who had imprisoned him after he was robbed of his strength at Delilah's betrayal. After regrowing his hair, the hero breaks his chains and topples the pillars of the temple, burying himself alive alongside thousands of his Philistine enemies. In a different version of this tale, the prophetess Deborah slays Sisera, commander of the opposing army, by hammering a tent stake through his head and crying: "So may all your enemies perish, Lord!"

The festival of Purim—which, due to its costumes, is often thought of here as a kind of Jewish Karneval—actually celebrates the Jewish victory over the evil royal vizier Haman: a servant of the Persian King Ahasuerus, who'd planned to murder the entire Jewish population of Persia. According to the Book of Esther, the story of Purim ends with the salvation of the Jewish community and an absolute bloodbath for Haman's followers. And each spring, to celebrate Pesach, the festival commemorating the exodus from Egypt, we ask God to take vengeance on all enemies of the Jewish people. The evening ceremony contains a strict, ceremonial succession of symbolic rituals: a leg of lamb to symbolize the sacrificial lamb in the Jewish temple; salt water for the tears shed by the Israelites under slavery in Egypt; and charoset, a fruit paste that symbolizes the mortar used by enslaved Jewish builders as they labored in Pithom and Raamses. The ceremony represents deliverance from oppression with the help of God. Another important aspect of the festival is freedom—which is represented by four full glasses of red wine and a chair—against which participants should lean with their left shoulder while drinking from the glasses: Free people sit comfortably. Pesach is a festival for remembering both the suffering and the anger of oppression. After eating, one repeats the following prayer:

Pour Your wrath upon the nations that did not know You and upon the kingdoms that did not call upon Your Name! Since they have consumed Jacob and laid waste his habitation. Pour out Your fury upon them and the fierceness of Your anger shall reach them! You shall pursue them with anger and eradicate them from under the skies of the Lord.

This prayer, excerpted from several psalms, is part of the Haggadah, and prescribes the order of events for the Pesach seder—which means that all participants in the ritual must repeat these lines. My edition of the *Haggadah* contains the following story beneath the aforementioned prayer:

> One day before Pesach in the year 1943, National Socialist military forces entered the Warsaw Ghetto to deport its inhabitants to Treblinka. Jewish resistance fighters repelled these soldiers, although they knew the troops would soon return with reinforcements. On this night, the Haggadah was recited to the accompaniment of gunshots and the explosions of grenades. The Jews cried as their rabbis began to sing: "Pour Your wrath upon the nations that did not know You . . . " (Shire, 46)

This brings me back to the memoires of Zipora Birman: I'm not surprised that people who experienced the horror of the murder of their entire families, congregations, shtetls, and cities began to think in apocalyptic, religious dimensions. In light of the scale of the German Wehrmacht's crimes and the thoroughness with which the German special forces oversaw the murder of the Jews, this kind of apocalyptic perspective even seems far more plausible to me than any attempts to try to identify some kind of normality or sense with this course of events. I am also reminded of the words of Hannah

Arendt from her conversation with Günter Gaus that I cited in Chapter 6, a conversation in which she goes on to describe how knowledge of the systematic annihilation of the Jewish people affected her, and how she responded to this knowledge philosophically:

> Before that, we said, well, one has enemies. That is natural. Why shouldn't people have enemies? But this was different. It was as if an abyss had opened. We had the idea that amends could be made for everything else. Amends can be made for almost anything at some point in politics. But not for this. This ought never to have happened. I don't just mean the number of victims. I mean what happened to the corpses. I need not go into detail. That should never have happened. Something happened to which we can never reconcile ourselves.

From a Jewish perspective, I believe that these acts of vengeance were a reasonable reaction to the things that had just happened. Immediately following its establishment, Abba Kovner's group, DIN, formulated two primary plans for revenge. The first was an attempt to poison the water supplies of major German cities, including Hamburg, Frankfurt am Main, Munich, and Nuremberg. Whether they knew it or not, these plans aligned with a long Christian tradition: the antisemitic cliché that Jews were poisoning Christian wells.

And as a consequence of the immense crimes committed against the Jewish people, now Jewish avengers really were planning to poison the wells. Not such a bad comeback at all. By 1945, members of the group had already infiltrated Nuremberg's municipal water supply, and were establishing how to shut off the water to the houses where Allied soldiers were being quartered—after all, these soldiers were not the targets of their vengeance. The plan collapsed, however, when Abba Kovner was arrested on a British warship on his return journey from a fundraising mission to Palestine. His companions threw the poison they had collected overboard. DIN's second plan revolved around a bakery in Langwasser, a district of Nuremberg where SS prisoners of war were being held captive. This bakery produced their rations of bread. During the night of April 13, 1946, three members of DIN forced their way into the bakery and smeared arsenic over nearly three thousand loaves of brown bread. One thousand nine hundred of the more than sixteen thousand prisoners at the concentration camp were poisoned. Many were hospitalized. But there were no fatalities.

Research on Jewish revenge is largely in agreement that—although thoughts of vengeance and anger did exist—most Jewish survivors sought other outlets for their feelings than did Abba Kovner and his followers. New York historian Atina Grossmann describes in her 2002 work how the extraordinarily high marriage and birth rates in the encampments that housed displaced persons after the War represented a form of revenge against the Nazis and their plans to exterminate Europe's Jews. Liliana Furman, the German program director for the American Jewish Joint Distribution Committee, and Liliana Ruth Feierstein, Professor of Transcultural Jewish History at the Humboldt-Universität zu Berlin, argue that thoughts of revenge played out primarily in the realm of Jewish literature after 1945. But while these more or less socially productive iterations of Jewish anger and the desire for vengeance might serve to alleviate the fears of German contemporaries, the idea that these Jewish desires were simply translated into babies and art doesn't present an accurate picture of what really happened.

In Israel, Yom Hashoah, the primary day for remembering the Shoah, was dedicated on the anniversary of the Warsaw Ghetto Uprising. And yet Jewish acts of vengeance that took place *after* World War II are still largely ignored. The US philosopher Berel Lang muses that one reason why these acts of vengeance tend to be ignored—even by Jewish postwar historians—is that aggressive acts can compromise the morally infallible image of victimhood that both Jewish and non-Jewish publics established after the Holocaust. A number of studies from the 1990s have demonstrated that our ignorance of these events has far more to do with a simple lack of public visibility than it does with the historical absence of such events. In 2000, the wide-ranging

German-language work *Nakam—Jüdische Rache an NS-Tätern* [Nakam—Jewish Revenge on NS Perpetrators] was published by the Nuremberg-based journalists and historians Jim G. Tobias and Peter Zinke—inspired by the aforementioned essay "Ende der Schonzeit" by Eike Geisel. But unlike in Israel, the two days of German-Jewish remembrance were established on November 9—the anniversary of the Nazi *Pogromnacht* of 1938, and January 27—the day on which Auschwitz was liberated in 1945. Both dates commemorate Jewish people as passive victims. Neither day recalls Jewish resistance *during* and against National Socialism. Tobias and Zinke observe: "To act as though Jewish people did not rise up against their own annihilation and retaliate against the Nazis reinforces the preconception that Jews were weak and helpless victims" (8–9). No doubt. And it is not by sheer coincidence that this preconception of Jewish people as victims presupposes one of the central Jewish figures in the German Theater of Memory. Representations of Jewish revenge, on the other hand, offer a powerful disruption to the staging of German-Jewish memory. After 1945, both historical and artistic representations of Jewish revenge play equally important roles in this—because physical and artistic vengeance become increasingly difficult to separate from one another. Especially when one considers the role that historical stereotypes played in real-life events. Just think of Abba Kovner's plan to poison the wells, or the effects of real-life antisemitism on the ongoing (re)formation of the Shylock figure from Shakespeare's *The Merchant of Venice*.

In fact, the motif of revenge provides a counternarrative across postwar Jewish art. I have already named a few key literary examples in the works of Paul Celan, Nelly Sachs, and Maxim Biller. A few others might include the diary entries of the poet Itzhak Katzenelson, Adorno's *Traumprotokolle* [Dream Protocols], the poetry of Thomas Brasch, or Zvi Kolitz's *Jossel Rakovers Wendung zu Gott* [Yossel Rakover Speaks to God]. Primo Levi, a Holocaust survivor and the author of the partisan novel *Wann, wenn nicht jetzt?* [If Not Now, When?], published the poem "Für Adolf Eichmann" [For Adolf Eichmann] in 1960, which is representative of broader expressions of Jewish vengeance in the postwar period. The following is an excerpt from Ruth Feldman and Brian Swann's translation of this poem:

FOR ADOLF EICHMANN

. . . And you have come, our precious enemy,
Forsaken creature, man ringed by death.
What can you say now, before our assembly?
Will you swear by a god? What god?
Will you leap happily into the grave?
Or will you at the end, like the industrious man

Whose life was too brief for his long art,
Lament your sorry work unfinished,
The thirteen million still alive?

Oh son of death, we do not wish you death.
May you live longer than anyone ever lived.
May you live sleepless five million nights,
And may you be visited each night by the suffering
    of everyone who saw,
Shutting behind him, the door that blocked the way
    back,
Saw it grow dark around him, the air fill with death.

                                         (24)

This poem stages revenge independent of any historical examples of Jewish vengeance, but real-life vengeance can also serve as a model for artistic processing. Detroit musician and poet Daniel Kahn dedicates his song "Six Million Germans" to Abba Kovner. The song was released in 2009 on the album *Partisans & Parasites*, and it contains the chorus:

Six Million Germans
You may think it was insane
Six Million Germans
That it was misdirected pain
Six Million Germans

They didn't want the war to end
Six Million Germans
They want one thing, *Nakham*: Revenge.

These lines already represent one break with Holocaust taboos, because the number six million is actually reserved for Jewish Shoah victims. When Daniel Kahn sings about six million Germans as the goal of Abba Kovner's revenge plot, he inverts the real historical relations. The peculiar comedy that he generates in this act is underscored by the pounding rhythm of the song itself. Just imagine a German audience dancing to this song and singing along to the chorus: "Six Million Germans!" Priceless.

Nevertheless, and despite these few examples, it remains indicative of the taboo nature of this subject among Jewish people that the most prominent artistic realization of Jewish revenge comes from the non-Jewish director Quentin Tarantino. His 2009 film *Inglourious Basterds* tells the story of a group of Jewish-American soldiers deployed behind enemy lines in France. Under the leadership of Lieutenant Aldo Raine (played by Brad Pitt), this Jewish brigade begins a brutal campaign of guerilla warfare to inspire fear and horror among the German soldiers. My personal favorite passage from the film comes from Aldo Raine's address to his troops, shortly before they are deployed in France. It is, for me, one of the pivotal works of revenge art:

My name is Lieutenant Aldo Raine, and I'm puttin' together a special team. And I need me eight soldiers. Eight-Jewish-American-soldiers. Now y'all might of heard rumors about the armada happening soon. Well, we'll be leavin' a little earlier. We're gonna be dropped into France, dressed as civilians. And once we're in enemy territory, as a bushwackin', guerilla army, we're gonna be doin' one thing, and one thing only—Killin' Nazis.

[. . .] Now I don't know 'bout y'all? But I sure as hell didn't come down from the goddamn Smoky Mountains, cross five thousand miles of water, fight my way through half Sicily, and then jump out of a fuckin' air-o-plane to teach the Nazis lessons in humanity. Nazi ain't got no humanity. They're the foot soldiers of a Jew-hatin', mass-murderin' maniac, and they need to be destroyed. That's why any and every son-of-a-bitch we find wearin' a Nazi uniform, they're gonna die.

We will be cruel to the Germans, and through our cruelty, they will know who we are. They will find the evidence of our cruelty in the disemboweled, dismembered, and disfigured bodies of their brothers we leave behind us. And the Germans will not be able to help themselves from imagining the cruelty their brothers endured at our hands, and our bootheels, and the edge of our knives. And the Germans will be sickened by us. And the Germans will talk about us. And the Germans will fear us. And when the Germans close their eyes at night and their subconscious tortures them for the evil they've done, it will be thoughts of us that it tortures them with.

The fact that acts of Jewish revenge remain in the background of Jewish narratives again demonstrates the extent to which Jewish self-perception—along with the way in which Jewish people are perceived by others—remains influenced by the Theater of Memory. At the same time, the many artistic reworkings of this subject provide evidence for the autonomy of Jewish discourse I've discussed in the preceding chapters. In principle, I agree with Liliana Furman and Liliana Ruth Feierstein that literature "[provides] a legitimate space for Jewish revenge, a humane and symbolic vengeance that makes it possible for feelings to be expressed and processed in this quiet moment between people and their actions" (182). But to me, the purpose of this insight does not seem to be for revenge art to serve as mere ritualization, but rather for the creation of spaces to express different Jewish positionalities after 1945. These works of art allow Jews not to serve solely as victims, but also as avenging angels: as the vanquishers of Nazi fascism.

Power to reinterpret alleged Jewish powerlessness can be drawn from Jewish tradition—from the many stories of vengeance that have also been incorporated into Jewish liturgy. But it can also be drawn from stories of Jewish revenge after World War II. And most surprisingly, perhaps, it can also be drawn from the tropes of antisemitic works themselves, such as Shylock in Shakespeare's *The Merchant of Venice* or the wealthy Jew in Fassbinder's *Der Müll, die Stadt und der Tod*. Strategies of reinterpreting discriminatory discourses have a long tradition among marginalized groups. The subgenre of rape and revenge films in feminist traditions (Reifenberger, *Girls with Guns*) or the violent rhetoric of many rap lyrics that invert the realities of social relations between the dominant culture and minoritized groups are but two examples of such reinterpretation.

It's one of the qualities of this revenge art that Jewish revenge—although perhaps destructive at first glance—isn't delegitimized, but rather employed for contemporary Jewish empowerment. Revenge art is a form of *Gegenwartsbewältigung* [overcoming the present]. At the same time, topoi of revenge also present a fundamentally destabilizing dimension for the Jewish perspective. Because when we surrender the position of the Good Victim, the Jewish subject is revealed as fragmentary, inscrutable, and unstable. In my play *Celan mit der Axt*, Amichai Süß says: "We're not the Good Victims, we're the evil ones." And because German-Jewish interactions serve not merely to stabilize the German self-image, but also to maintain the stability and clarity of the Jewish positionality, references to Jewish revenge not only destabilize the ascription of roles in the German Theater of Memory, but also destabilize many Jewish people's own self-conception.

The difficulty of stabilizing one's own, oft-shattered Jewish identity is one reason why so many Jewish people find themselves identifying with external ascriptions again and again. And I am well aware of how uncomfortable it is to realize that one has internalized external clichés and fantasies about oneself. Exploring revenge art is one way of processing these internalized clichés. And this is a prerequisite for an effective critique of the Theater of Memory.

Two generations of mourning, trauma, and fear lie behind us. And it took some doing, but now we're back. This is Jew Sour.* These are the Inglourious Poets. We won the War. And this time, the Germans won't get away so easily.

---

* *Jud Sauer*: a play on the 1925 historical novel *Jud Süß* [Jew Sweet] by Jewish author Lion Feuchtwanger.

11

AHASVER'S HELL: OR, THINGS WILL NEVER BE "ALL GOOD" AGAIN

RECENTLY, THERE'S BEEN a good deal of discussion about the deaths of first-generation Holocaust survivors. The primary question seems to be: How do we continue to remember the Shoah after this first generation of witnesses is dead? When they can no longer roll up their sleeves and show us the identification numbers tattooed on their arms? But what I never hear in these lamentations is any word about the deaths of the first-generation perpetrators. What is the significance of the death of an entire generation who might have been—but (by overwhelming majority) were not—held legally accountable for their crimes? Does the history of National Socialism end with the biological end of this generation of old Nazis? Is it as simple as that?

At this point, it probably will not surprise you, my highly esteemed readers, that I'm not satisfied with this. Even as a small child, I had violent dreams. I lay in bed imagining hacking off the arms of Nazi soldiers, kicking them to the curb, gathering a stockpile of weapons, and holding their forces at bay. I dreamed of killing Hitler, Goebbels, and their whole concentration camp team. I never fantasized about making everything "all good" again. I dreamed about fighting back. Hitting harder. If I couldn't stop what had happened, I at least wanted my revenge. Don't get me wrong, I'm not against reparations or special retirement funds. The wealth that German companies like Siemens, Deutsche Bank, Krupp, or the Deutsche Bahn accumulated and continue to profit from today are based in no small part on the dispossessed wealth of Jewish people and the forced labor of concentration camps. With these fond childhood memories, I'm trying to illustrate that—given the current state of affairs—I have absolutely no desire for normalization. I don't share in this elation about a "New Germany." Perhaps that's because I view the annihilation of my own people as a fundamental grievance. You can't make up for that with monuments and holidays.

Just a few decades ago, the overwhelming majority of Germans decided that they had no problem with marking their fellow citizens as Jews and then excluding, dispossessing, and murdering them. Even those who weren't turning the cranks at the gas chambers or filling up mass graves still had no problem taking over unfilled jobs, moving into the empty apartments—reading the books and eating with the cutlery of their previous inhabitants. When Germans of my generation tell me that they've had enough of Holocaust remembrances, I perceive this as a continuation of the same insult. As a lack of respect for my dead. For me, the "German homeland" [*deutsche Heimat*] is an ambivalent, violent, and traumatic place. Already in my youth, I learned that songs and poems could provide a language for expressing my grievances with German society. And for this reason alone, the works I discuss in Chapter 10 were incredibly influential to me. Like a rope lowered into the abyss within me that I could descend, only to reemerge with poetry.

For a long time, I struggled to find the right means for providing artistic expression for the anger I felt at the injustices that had been done to me and my family. I found them in unexpected places. I began to research the early history of Christian antisemitism for an academic paper. I was particularly interested in the origins of religious justifications for hostility toward Jews—which can, at least in part, be traced back to claims that God has banished them. Jesus, the son of God, condemned the Jewish people to eternal punishment and servitude because they had not acknowledged his divinity. This motif of divine punishment also finds expression in the High Medieval legend of the eternally wandering Jew, Ahasver, who had mocked Jesus on the way to his crucifixion. According to the story, Jesus asked a Jewish man for a sip of water on the way to Golgotha. When this man refused and, instead, began to taunt Jesus, Jesus cursed him: "I shall stand and rest, but thou shalt go on till the last day!" And so a central topos of the Jew figure in Christian antisemitism was born: the restless and wandering Jew, doomed forever to roam the Earth until Jesus' Second Coming delivers him from his wanderings.

The so-called "Ahasver Legend" first appears in a text by the English monk Roger of Wendover from the beginning of the thirteenth century. It was popularized in a German-language context after the 1602 publication of *Kurtzen Beschreibung und Erzehlung von einem Juden mit Namen Ahaßverus* [A Short Description and Tale of a Jew Named Ahassverus]. In 1694, with the first mention of the "Eternal Jew" [*Ewiger Jude*], this myth began to enter the works of a great number of German-language authors (Czollek, "Inglourious Poets"). Schubart, Goethe, Schiller, Schlegel, and Brentano all took up the Ahasver tale in the eighteenth century. The story developed differently outside the German-language context, and the Jewish figure went by any number of different names: Joannes Buttadeus, Cartaphilus, Malchus, Juan Espera-en-Dios. This happened, in part, due to connections with different aspects of regionally specific forms of antisemitism. While the image of the "Eternal Jew" became established in the German-speaking world, his English or French-language counterpart was often known as the "Wandering Jew" or "*juif errant.*" In his literary formulations, Ahasver was often a simple traveler, but he was also a rabble-rouser, a revolutionary ideal, or a symbolic figure to represent Judaism as such. The relative flexibility in terms of the actual contents of this myth allowed it to encapsulate numerous religious, political, social, philosophical, and cultural ideas. In its variety and contradictions, it became a classic case study for the various antisemitic indictments against "the Jews."

I find the legend of Ahasver particularly relevant when it comes to the part about the curse—suddenly Jesus appears like a magician, pronounces abracadabra, and Jews are condemned to eternal wandering. It seems to me that this central tenet of Christian hostility toward Jews collides here with a concept of linguistic performance: the idea that language produces realities. The implication—when it comes to antisemitism—is that this performance constitutes or even creates realities by labeling Jewish people variously as Communist firebrands, capitalist exploiters, knaves without a fatherland, or whatever else it might be. This reality is then manifest—or manifests itself—in political practices extending from questions of citizenship to pogroms to Auschwitz. If Jesus could really condemn the Jews to eternal wandering through one exchange with a Jewish man at the side of the road, this single incident represents a microcosm of the way in which antisemitic thought functions in its totality.

To put this differently: performativity means that social realities necessitate their own continual repetition *in practice*. There is no German self-conception without the Theater of Memory. There is no guiding culture without the Theater of Integration. Over the last decades, various strategies of intervention against this kind of repetition have become instruments in the toolbox of critical leftist practice. The highly influential works of Berkeley philosopher and linguist Judith Butler helped provide substance by proposing the idea that performative irritations can influence seemingly unalterable, established, identitarian roles. So, if antisemitism—like rigid patterns of gender identity or the Theaters of Memory and Integration—can become reality through continual perform-ance, could a critical Jewish intervention not develop out of the appropriation and reworking of a myth such as that of the Wandering Jew Ahasver? In my second collection of poetry, *Jubeljahre* [Jubilees], I set about identifying possible antecedents for this kind of strategy of the poetic re-processing of liter-ary material that might intervene in or invert the dominant perspective. I reencountered Heinrich Heine's *Deutschland. Ein Wintermärchen* at this time, and found myself captivated by one of its final passages. In Caput XXVII, Heine writes:

O king! I have your wellbeing at heart,
And there is the advice I give:
Honour the poets, who are dead,
But watch your step with those who live.

Do not offend the living poets,
For the weapons and flames in their possession,

Are deadlier than Jove's lightning,
Which was a poet's invention.

Offend the Gods, both old and new,
Offend the whole Olympian lot,
Plus mighty Jehovah, on top of them,
But the poet, offend him not!

Heine had already called it back in 1844: As a king, you can insult everyone—even God—because in the end, you will still be saved by Jesus. But even kings should fear the poet:

Yet, there are hells from whose confines
It is not possible to be freed.
No prayers can help, the Redeemer's pardon,
Even that! Will not succeed.

Have you ever heard of Dante's hell,
With its frightful verses and rhyme?
Whoever the poet imprisons there,
No God can ever free on time.

No God, no Saviour can deliver him
From those flames that burn.
Beware! O king and better behave,
For soon may well be your turn!

Those who receive the poet's wrath must face Dante's inferno, reopening its gates work by work, book by book, edition by edition. There can be no escape. And there are plenty of reasons why I love this passage. Firstly, because it takes literary worlds seriously: It is written, therefore it is real! Abracadabra! Secondly, because Heine adopts a position here that I otherwise know only from hip-hop battle rap. Someday, I'd like to see someone sit down and write a cultural history of battle rap dating back to the works of all-stars like Friedrich Nietzsche, Arthur Schopenhauer, Rudolf Carnap, Ludwig Wittgenstein, Hannah Arendt, Kurt Tucholsky, Bertolt Brecht, Elfriede Jelinek, and MC Heine. But this passage becomes even more interesting in context because Heine threatens kings with banishment into the realm of mythology and legend. He conceptualizes poetry as a place in which different forms of justice can be realized than those that exist in our daily lives.

Which brings me back to my opening question: Does the history of National Socialism end with the physical demise of geriatric Nazis? I don't think it does. National Socialism doesn't lose its impact on contemporary political discourses simply because a few old men and women die. There are the many ongoing continuities I've examined in previous chapters on one side, but from a Jewish perspective, I also really can't celebrate the fact that the death of first-generation Nazis also represents the return to normality for German self-conception. Whatever that even means. According to Jewish tradition, God continues to exact punishment for evil deeds over ten generations—just as God will reward good deeds over one hundred generations. Legal responsibilities may expire, but there are other kinds of responsibilities that supersede them. And we are only the third generation, after all.

I have no doubt that the perpetrators of the twentieth century's many crimes have earned themselves entry into Dante's inferno. And so I feel that it's high time to cash in on Heine's threat. And that was precisely what I was trying to do when I wrote the poetry cycle *A.H.A.S.V.E.R.* This cycle addresses several different aspects of this potentiality. Of course, the title references one of the many names of the legendary Wandering Jew. And in doing so, it takes on a myth that has influenced the European Christian imaginary of the Jew for nearly a thousand years. And the literary processing of material from this myth also has a long tradition from the Jewish perspective. The 1981 novel *Ahasver* by Stefan Heym is one twentieth-century example. But, like every other literary reworking of this myth that I can think of, Heym's Ahasver is also a Jewish figure.

In my cycle of poetry, Ahasver is no longer a Jew. Instead, this curse is laid upon a figure who is variously named Josef, Joseph, or Josif—a figure who oscillates between Joseph Goebbels and Joseph Stalin. The reader accompanies Josef over the course of nine poems, as he drifts between different mythological realities. The biblical story of Jacob and his ladder transforms into a memory of Goebbels' "Total War"

185

speech at the Sportpalast. The story of Jesus' crucifixion merges with a scene of the Holocaust in Eastern Europe. Magda Goebbels murdering her six children as Medea . . . I wanted to write this new Ahasver into the cosmology of European myth—myths through which Josef wanders eternally. The cycle of poems ends without the promise of salvation from the original Ahasver legend—an intervention born of the particularity of the twentieth century's crimes. In Christian tradition, Jesus' Second Coming serves as the prerequisite for the Jews to be freed from their eternal wandering. But because those murdered in the Shoah will never return, the eternal wanderings of Josef transpire without hope for a future salvation. This separates his tradition from that of the Wandering Jew.

A.H.A.S.V.E.R. represents a kind of mythological exchange of prisoners: the eternal Wandering Jew swapped out for the antisemites Stalin and Goebbels. And so this antisemitic myth is turned against its own creators, condemning them to literary hell. That's my kind of revenge. The voices of the Bear Jew and Abba Kovner, Meir Kahane and Primo Levi, Henry Morgenthau and the Kosher Nostra speak through it. Against the backdrop of Jewish de-integration, artistic revenge offers a dual intervention in the Theater of Memory. The first part is a form of self-empowerment: Antisemites are condemned to eternal wandering. The second part ensures an ongoing negotiation: When contrasted with the desire for normalization and *Vergangenheitsbewältigung* [overcoming the past] espoused by descendants of the perpetrators, this story offers no reconciliation.

I have already described how much I dislike the self-righteousness with which some Germans denounce their willingness to engage with remembrance as though this were self-evident: "I'm not responsible for my grandparents' crimes." Yeah, yeah: I'll be right back, I just need to get another beer. But instead, I go to the bathroom and doom-scroll through the latest misadventures of the Deutsche Bahn—which, by the way, seriously proposed naming one of its trains "Anne Frank" in 2018. They didn't see what the big deal was. And so, yes: I'm still pissed off about this cute new form of nationalism being advertised on every other product since 2006: Have a Coke for Germany! What a joke. What an arrogant, misplaced hope. As if somehow, somewhere, sometime things will just go back to normal.

I'd like to propose an amendment to the so-called "eternity clause" of the German constitution: *Things will never be "all good" again.*

12

THE BEGINNING IS NIGH: *DE-INTEGRATSIЯ*

THINGS HAVE BEEN going well for Germany. At the beginning of 2018, the employment office [*Agentur für die Arbeit*] reported over a billion-dollar surplus for the 2017 fiscal year—due, at least in part, to the fact that unemployment rates were at their lowest point since Reunification. The economy was booming and the newly arrived refugees contributed to the middle-term availability of a cheap, well-trained, and well-educated workforce. Germany had won the 2014 World Cup. It remained among the highest-ranked export nations. It earned an additional trophy for its talent in the cultural memory game, as well. It was like low tide before a hurricane. And during this time of relative stability, the far-right, nationalist AfD would go on to win just under 13 percent of the vote in the 2017 federal election—propelling the radical Right from relative obscurity to the third-most represented party in the Bundestag, with representation from fourteen of Germany's sixteen federal states. So what happens when the next economic crisis arrives?[*] And we can be sure that it will, because since the end of the so-called Cold War, capitalism has not, exactly, enacted a new phase of sustainable development.

And so while we scratch our bellies and wait for the next storm waves to roll in, the extreme Right has been modernizing its political playbook. They are, again, very much part of the German political establishment. Proud Germans! Wrapped in a new rhetorical costume, the CDU and CSU have combined forces with the AfD to reestablish a new (old) program for German nationalism. The Ministry of *Heimat* is now the official term for the Ministry of the Interior on a federal level. Ah, how I wish I'd someday be able to boast as many print runs and reissues for my books as the forces for rebranding German nationalism can. Meanwhile, the SPD, the Green Party, and Die Linke have all reacted by trying to recast themselves as positive incarnations of this *Heimat* movement by simultaneously seeking to court AfD voters while kindly demanding the immediate integration of refugees.

The things happening in this country today are nothing new. This cannot be explained away by a general rightward populist swing in European politics. When we think,

---

[*] For an analysis of Germany's current sociopolitical state in the pandemic era, you'll have to learn German and read *Gegenwartsbewältigung* (Hanser 2021). Or wait for another English translation!

today, about PEGIDA and the AfD, we mustn't forget that Martin Walser had referred to the Holocaust Memorial as the "monumentalization of shame" in 1998. We mustn't forget the xenophobic arson attacks of the 1990s and the burning of asylum homes at the hands of neo-Nazi terrorists—just like today, people pointed to the rising number of refugees then like it was some kind of apology. Rather than combating these provocations by cracking down on rightwing violence, their increasing frequency led to the revision and restriction of Article 16 of the German constitution in 1992—an article that had guaranteed the absolute right of asylum to those fleeing political persecution since 1949. The SPD was part of the opposition then, but on May 26, 1993, these amendments were approved with the combined votes of the CDU, CSU, and FDP. And the neo-Nazis thanked these politicians for their support by burning two Turkish families alive in their homes in Solingen just two days later (Utlu, "Für Trauer," 4). We also mustn't forget West Germany's so-called "*Radikalenbeschluss*" [radical resolution] of 1972, which aimed to restrict leftwing activists from public service or public office. And we should remember that by the mid-1950s, nearly all Nazis had been rehabilitated back into civil life from their prior positions in the National Socialist administration or military. Things were the same but different in the German Democratic Republic, where the Party made sure that antisemitic incidences were covered up as quickly and as quietly as possible. When we look back at the social and legal legacy of the past seventy years, it becomes difficult to construe this period as a successful conquest over National Socialism. Instead, things start to look a lot more like its successful integration.

The AfD may have only recently succeeded in establishing its presence in the Bundestag, but its foundation lies in an uninterrupted tradition of political thought and political recognition: nationalism, obsessive love for the German *Heimat*, and its concept of *Volksverbundenheit* [ethnonational affinity]. Normality in this country cannot be reduced to the reappearance of German flags and miles of jubilant soccer fans before the Brandenburg Gate—it is also deeply intertwined with *völkisch*-ethnonationalism and attacks on refugee asylum homes. Rightwing thought takes on unique qualities and characteristics in Germany. And because of that, this book is also a vigorous appeal for more *abnormality*. A plea. We have to break the cycle of this yearning for so-called normality.

I've argued that explanations for the reemergence of the Far Right miss the point as long as they fail to recognize continuities and the influence that National Socialism continues to exercise over present-day German society—nearly three-quarters of a century after its defeat. With representatives of a *völkisch*-ethnonationalist party sitting in the Bundestag and the increasing normalization of conservative-rightwing positions in political parties, feuilletons, and general public life, these continuities are becoming more visible by the day.

And it is no coincidence that people find it so difficult to recognize the underlying truths within the present situation: Continuity with National Socialism is incongruous to the new German self-image. Germans are prepared for everything—everything but recognizing themselves as part of a society descended from Nazis.

So why am I talking about the Theater of Memory anyway? Doesn't twenty-first-century Germany treat its Jews well? Aren't I too young to be worried about this anyway? I get these kinds of questions the moment I become careless enough to start discussing German-Jewish relations with strangers. But these are all just poorly concealed invitations to finally play along with the game called *Everything Is Back to Normal!* These kinds of invitations were already embedded in the questions those reporters asked us at the Jewish School: Do you feel welcome here? The Theater of Memory is also at play in the way people regard my artistic work as a poet, playwright, and publicist. Jews are ascribed roles that help stabilize the new German self-image: the forgiving Jewish victims on one side and the reformed German perpetrators on the other.

I need de-integration for my own artistic autonomy. But the Theater of Memory is also a structural problem. What we celebrate today as a living Jewish community in Germany is largely the result of social engineering: an expression of the will of the German government after Reunification. Because the presence of Jewish people from the (post-)Soviet world—a demographic that today represents 90 percent of Germany's Jewish population—exists purely due to the political decision to allow this wave of (im)migrants. *Cui bono?* Of course, this act of generosity also represented the desires of a portion of those representatives of extant Jewish communities in East and West Germany. But at the same time, immigration performed a function in reinforcing Reunified German society's self-conception, as well. The existence of a contemporary Jewish community in Germany—and here, perhaps, it *does* make sense to speak of a generic "community"—is also the result of the German desire to *produce* a Jewish community.

In Chapter 9, I've tried to describe how Jewish migration over the last decades has also produced new forms of Jewish diversity that make a strategy like de-integration possible in the first place. Unlike the first generation of survivors (and their immediate descendants), the current generation no longer depends on recognition by German dominant culture. On the one hand, this is due to demographic developments, but it also has something to do with the growing artistic and political autonomy of Jewish people in Germany today. I've tried to emphasize Jewish narratives and Jewish perspectives that may help us develop alternatives to the Theater of Memory. I've also highlighted the dazzling potential for irony and revenge to interrupt the well-established relations between Germans and Jews. These are all starting points for Jewish de-integration.

But this newfound Jewish autonomy does not change the fact that the mere existence of Jewish life in Germany—a country that in living memory attempted to exterminate its Jews—*does* do something to alleviate the desire for exoneration. As a Jewish critic of German-Jewish relations, one inevitably descends into a flurry of self-contradictions. And, of course, this applies to the book you currently hold in your hands, as well. I can't deny that one of the most obvious of these contradictions is the fact that a book like this—to a certain degree—also reproduces the process by which human beings are reduced into representatives of Jewishness for public consumption. At the same time, I am convinced that it's unavoidable that problems are reproduced the moment we call them out. If I've presented Germans and Jews in binary opposition throughout this book, this is because the Theater of Memory creates these distinctions between Germans and Jews. And certainly, I have attempted to update this differentiation and critique the unequal power dynamics of this binary. And in that regard, I'd like to defend my own position with another quote (and question) from the indefatigable Jewish philosopher Hannah Arendt: "If one is attacked as a Jew, one must defend oneself as a Jew. Not as a German or a world citizen. Or an upholder of human rights. But what could I do specifically as a Jew?" I don't believe that there is any real escape from the Theater of Memory without a larger, fundamental shift in the way the majority of people in this country conceive of the society in which they live. And this depends equally on a critique of both the Theater of Memory and the integration paradigm. Following the 2017 federal election, one could calculate that 87.4 percent of voters chose *not* to vote for the AfD. And I guess that should sound reassuring. But that would depend on how or whether this other 87.4 percent took any appropriate political action. Such political actions, such consequences, must result in the formation of entirely new concepts and alliances. And the possibility of *this* is precluded by the endurance of the integration paradigm.

The idea of complete and total integration of everything and everybody is nothing more than a disposable projection screen for German fantasies of cultural dominance. Its founding fantasy of a bourgeois social middle ground renders the full recognition of the radical diversity of contemporary German society impossible. But this radical diversity is already social reality. Nevertheless, Germany's new Antisemitism Commissioner declared in 2018 that Germany can only conceptualize itself as a partner of the Jews. And not as a country whose population is partly Jewish. And as long as this kind of integration is taken up by the political mainstream, my friends and I will not take part in it. But our participation is critical.

Because a tidal wave is approaching—and unlike most of the talking heads you'll hear from in Germany these days, I'm not talking about the growing number of refugees. I mean the rising water levels in the sewer systems of German history.

And in order to survive the cesspools spilling over, those who defend our pluralist society will have to mobilize all the powers they've got. The search for new alliances is not a question of fun, or the preoccupation of an internationalist *Multikulti.*[*] It's a necessity. Defending social pluralism means upholding this *ongoing* work for an open society. There is a myriad of open sewer drains—and when I look at the coalition platform for our current government, it doesn't inspire confidence that they will be closed any time soon.

One pressing requirement for the formation of new alliances lies in the recognition of the acute, existential threats that are being leveled against far too many people in Germany today. According to the Amadeu Antonio Foundation and Pro Asyl, there was an average of four attacks per day against refugees in 2017. In the same year, the Federal Criminal Police Office registered 251 attacks. That's one attack per work day, if we calculate according to the public holiday schedule in the state of Berlin. But terrorists like the National Socialist Underground and rightwing arsonists are merely the executive force of a deep-seated, socially engrained racism. It is unthinkable that such shocking numbers would be politically acceptable against a different demographic group. Imagine ecoterrorists in this country committing daily attacks on diesel

---

[*]   A kitsch talking point for the liberal, centrist imaginary of multi-culturalism in Germany.

auto-repair shops. There would be dragnet investigations and home raids quicker than I can type the words "inner-city fine particulate air pollution." And I'd like to see a German president advise the auto industry to make cleaner cars if they'd like to avoid this kind of problem in the future. Do you see where I'm going with this analogy?

Germany's history has been interpreted as the trauma of a belated national identity—but it could also be read as a story of inter-German plurality. Because, historically, there has never once existed anything like a clearly defined German guiding culture. And there isn't one today either. The area on which present-day Germany is located was—for most of its history—a patchwork quilt of various tribes and petty principalities with a great diversity of lifestyles, dialects, religions, and senses of belonging and shared identification. These differences didn't simply disappear with the founding of the (Prussian) German state in 1871. There have also been numerous large-scale waves of (im)migration, including those that took place after both World War II and German Reunification. Germany's historical diversity could provide an occasion to fundamentally rethink the society we live in—and the society we *want* to live in today.

In the 1879 essay "Unsere Aussichten" [Our Views], renowned historian, nationalist, and antisemite Heinrich von Treitschke outlines his demands on Germany's Jewish population—a population who had first received the rights of citizenship just eight years earlier, after the Prussian Wars of Unification:

> What we require of our Israelite citizens is easy: They should become Germans. They should quite simply feel that they are Germans—without prejudice to their beliefs and their ancient, holy memories that are venerable to all of us. For we do not wish for the thousands of years of Germanic civilization to be followed by an era of German-Jewish cultural mix. (573)

The book you hold in your hands is a plea for the preservation of precisely this kind of "cultural mix." An appeal for Jewish-Muslim hegemony. I believe that discussions of who belongs in Germany (and who doesn't) are the expression of an immoderate and invasive arrogance that should not be spared a comparison with the garbage philosophies of Heinrich von Treitschke. Even in his time, those "thousands of years of Germanic civilization" were nothing more than a dangerous self-delusion. And they remain a delusion, even when contemporary politicians rebrand them as thousands of years of "Judeo-Christian" tradition. I really would find these kinds of claims hilarious if I didn't have to constantly defend myself against them. Because I simply can't accept that another religion is, *again*, being excluded from German society today—even when this time it's not the Jewish faith.

And obviously, an all-encompassing alliance between Germany's Jewish and Muslim populations seems unlikely. Antisemitism and Islamophobia inhibit our cooperation. And a lot of Jewish people today would like to believe that they will never again fall victim to systemic persecution at the hands of German politicians. I think this, too, is a delusion. Next time, the mosques might be the first to burn. But then the synagogues will burn, as well. I don't entertain any illusions about this.

Although he seems to have misplaced his moral compass in the meantime, in 1994 US publicist Leon Wieseltier described an important prerequisite for the formation of new alliances. In his essay "Against Identity," Wieseltier argues that we need to move beyond the imaginary of clearly delineated identity, free from all contradictions—a notion that has become so central to current cultural-political debates. We should, instead, become more conscientious of our own inner fragmentation—the incongruities that comprise each individual. Because identity is not only an instrument for defending ourselves against becoming instrumentalized by a given dominant culture. It is also something monolithic, something dogmatic, and something deeply unironic. The Turkish-Armenian journalist Hrant Dink, who was himself murdered by Turkish nationalists writes: "If you can only maintain your own identity as conceived by your enemies, then this identity becomes a sickness" (Popp, "Schuld ohne Sühne"). If we truly wish to form new alliances, we also need to move away from identitarian ideals of belonging to one particular group: away from the idea that our identities are something whole and self-defining, and that we must fight to defend their integrity. Every human being is composed of many shifting pieces. The unfractured identity is a dangerous illusion.

I would like to end with this (potentially) surprisingly inclusive outlook. Many years and many conversations, many lengthy reading lists, much anger and much divergent and often unexpected reinforcement lie between my own first impulses for de-integration five years ago, and the months in which I sat at various desks and wrote this book. Without these many encounters, I would not have been able to do it. And for that reason, I would like to thank not merely those who have encouraged and reinforced me, but also those whose provocations inspired my resistance. I think both sides contributed equally to this polemic.

So ultimately, the invocation in this book's German title, *Desintegriert euch!* [De-Integrate Yourselves!], remains just as true in its inversion: De-Integrate Me!

ACKNOWLEDGMENTS

I'd like to thank Leah Carola Czollek, Jonas Fegert, Jo Frank, Daniel Graf, Corinne Kaszner, Vera Lorenz, Gudrun Perko, Sasha Salzmann, Deniz Utlu, and Uwe Wolf for their many helpful comments and suggestions. Thank you, Florian Kessler, for your attentive readership. And special thanks to the Kulturakademie Tarabya Istanbul for providing me the opportunity as Writer-in-Residence to finish this book.

I also want to thank my US publisher, Restless Books, for making this work available in English. I owe the greatest thanks to my translator, Jon Cho-Polizzi, whom I first met in a meadow in a little village in the Black Forest and got to know in those endless Berlin nights between parks and bars. The struggle continues, my friend.

BIBLIOGRAPHY

"9. November 1938: Joachim Gauck erinnert an die Opfer der Pogromnacht." *Frankfurter Rundschau.* November 9, 2015. https://www.rundschau-online.de/politik/9--november-1938-joachim-gauck-erinnert-an-die-opfer-der-pogromnacht-23082446.

Adorno, Theodor W. "Prismen—Kulturkritik und Gesellschaft." In *Kulturkritik und Gesellschaft I—Gesammelte Schriften*, vol. 10.1. Edited by Rolf Tiedemann. Darmstadt: Wissenschaftliche Buchgesellschaft, 1998.

——. *Traumprotokolle*. Frankfurt am Main: Suhrkamp, 2005.

Althusser, Louis. "Ideologie & ideologische Staatsapparate." In *Ideologie und ideologische Staatsapparate. Aufsätze zur marxistischen Theorie*. Hamburg: VSA, 1977. 108-53.

Aly, Götz. *Unser Kampf 1968—ein irritierter Blick zurück*. Frankfurt am Main: Fischer, 2008.

Amann, Melanie. *Angst für Deutschland. Die Wahrheit über die AfD: wo sie herkommt, wer sie führt, wohin sie steuert*. Munich: Droemer Knaur Verlag, 2017.

Arendt, Hannah. "'What Remains? The Language Remains': A conversation with Günter Gaus." Translated by Joan Stambaugh. In *The Last Interview and Other Conversations*. New York: Melville House, 2013. 7–41. Video of original interview (from the *Zur Person* television program, 1964): https://youtube.com/watch?v=J9SyTEUi6Kw.

Ayata, Imran. "Heute die Gesichter, morgen die Ärsche." *SPEX* 11 (1999): http://www.kanak-attak.de/ka/text/spex1199. html.

Ayim, May. *Blues in Schwarz-Weiß*. Berlin: Orlanda Frauenverlag, 1996.

BAMF. "Online-Glossar des BAMF." https://www.bamf.de/DE/ Service/Left/Glossary/_function/glossar.html?lv3=1504494& lv2=5831826 [no longer available].

——. "Welcome to Germany." https://www.bamf.de/SharedDocs/ Anlagen/EN/Integration/WillkommenDeutschland/ willkommen-in-deutschland.pdf?__blob=publicationFile &v=21.

Bauer, Katja. "Felix Klein wird erster Antisemitismusbeauftragter." *Stuttgarter Zeitung*. April 11, 2018. https://www.stuttgarter-zeitung.de/inhalt.ansprechpartner-fuer-juedisches-leben-felix- klein-wird-erster-antisemitismusbeauftragter.5dfa7 2a9-ea16-49d8-9602-3227ca445fad.html.

Belkin, Dmitrij. "'Yolocaust'. Ahistorische Leere." *Jüdische Allgemeine*. January 26, 2017. http://www.juedische-allgemeine.de/article/view/id/27625.

Belkin, Dmitrij, and Raphael Gross. *Ausgerechnet Deutschland! Jüdisch-russische Einwanderung in die Bundesrepublik*. Berlin: Nicolai'sche Verlagsbuchhandlung, 2010.

Biller, Maxim. *Der gebrauchte Jude. Ein Selbstportrait*. Cologne: Kiepenheuer & Witsch, 2009.

——. "Heiliger Holocaust." *Die Zeit*. November 8, 1996. http:// www.zeit.de/1996/46/bill46.19961108.xml/komplettansicht.

——. "Wenn ich einmal reich und tot bin." In *100 Zeilen Hass: Erstmals komplett*. Hamburg: Hoffmann und Campe Verlag, 2017. Previously published in *Wenn ich einmal reich und tot bin*. Cologne: Kiepenheuer & Witsch, 1990.

Bodemann, Y. Michal. "Die Endzeit der Märtyrer-Gründer. An einer Epochenwende jüdischer Existenz in Deutschland." *Babylon* 8 (1991).

——. *Gedächtnistheater. Die jüdische Gemeinschaft und ihre deutsche Erfindung*. Hamburg: Rotbuch, 1996.

Böttiger, Helmut. "Die Wahrheit über Paul Celans Auftritt bei der Gruppe 47." *Deutschlandfunk Kultur*, May 21, 2017. http://www.deutschlandfunkkultur.de/lesung-im-jahr-1952-die-wahrheit-ueber-paul-celans-auftritt.974.de.html?dram:article_id=386529.

Broder, Henryk M. "Antisemitismus—ja bitte." *Süddeutsche Zeitung*. January 18. 1986.

——. *Der ewige Antisemit: Über Sinn und Funktion eines beständigen Gefühls*. Berlin: Fischer, 1986.

——. "Ihr bleibt die Kinder Eurer Eltern." *Die Zeit*. February 21, 1981. http://www.zeit.de/1981/10/ihr-bleibt-die-kinder-eurer-eltern.

——. "So schafft man den Antisemitismus juristisch ab." *welt.de*, October 15, 2014. https://www.welt.de/kultur/article133303492/So-schafft-man-den-Antisemitismus-juristisch-ab.html.

Brothers Keepers. "Adriano—letzte Warnung." Directed by Dani Levy. 2001. Music video, 7:07. https://www.youtube.com/watch?v=xXawL-LFgi8.

Brumlik, Micha. "Juden, Judentum und Rechtspopulismus." *Jalta* 2 (2017): 132–34.

Butler, Judith. *Bodies That Matter: On the Discursive Limits of "Sex."* New York: Routledge, 1993.

"Chronik flüchtlingsfeindlicher Vorfälle." *Mut Gegen Rechte Gewalt*. https://www.mut-gegen-rechte-gewalt.de/service/chronik-vorfaelle.

Coleman, Arica L. "James Baldwin Documentary *I Am Not Your Negro* Is the Product of a Specific Moment in History." *time.com* February 24, 2017. http://time.com/4680673/james-baldwin-documentary-history/.

Czollek, Max. "Inglourious Poets. Rache als Topos jüdischer Selbstermächtigung." In *A.H.A.S.V.E.R.* Berlin: Verlagshaus Berlin, 2015.

——. "Celan mit der Axt." Unpublished play. 2017.

Czollek, Max, Corinne Kaszner, Leah Carola Czollek, and Gudrun Perko. "Radical Diversity und Desintegration. Bausteine eines künstlerisch-politischen Projekts." *Jalta* 2 (2017): 71–78.

"'Der Islam gehört nicht zu Deutschland'. Was will Seehofer mit diesem Satz erreichen?" *Bild*, March 16, 2018. https://www.bild.de/politik/inland/horst-seehofer/was-will-er-mit-seinem-interview-erreichen-55120448.bild.html.

Destasis. "Bevölkerung mit Migrationshintergrund um 8,5 % gestiegen." August 1, 2017. https://www.destatis.de/DE/PresseService/Presse/Pressemitteilungen/2017/08/PD17_261_12511.html.

"Dichterin Nora Gomringer bekommt Ringelnatz-Preis für Lyrik." *Evangelisch-Lutherischer Sprengel Hildesheim-Göttingen*. April 17, 2012. https://sprengelhildesheimgoettingen.wordpress.com/2012/04/17/auschwitz-gedicht-und-es-war-ein-tag/#more-2797 [no longer available].

Diner, Dan. "Negative Symbiose. Deutsche und Juden nach Auschwitz." *Babylon* 1 (1986): 9–20.

Dobrindt, Alexander. "Wir brauchen eine bürgerlich-konservative Wende." *Die Welt*, January 4, 2018. https://www.welt.de/debatte/kommentare/article172133774/Warum-wir-nach-den-68ern- eine-buergerlich-konservative-Wende-brauchen.html.

Eco, Umberto. *Im Wald der Fiktionen*, Munich: dtv, 1996.

"Entzug des Bleiberechts für antisemitische Migranten gefordert." *Jüdische Allgemeine*. April 9, 2018. http://www.juedische-allgemeine.de/article/view/id/31237.

Enzensberger, Hans Magnus. "Die Steine der Freiheit." *Merkur* 138 (August 1959): 772.

Eribon, Didier. *Rückkehr nach Reims*. Translated by Tobias Haberkorn. Berlin: De Gruyter, 2016.

"Expertenkreis ohne Juden. Heftige Kritik an der Zusammensetzung der Antisemitismus-Kommission des Innenministeriums." *Jüdische Allgemeine*, February 10, 2015. http://www.juedische-allgemeine.de/article/view/id/21497.

Fassbinder, Rainer Werner. "Der Müll, die Stadt und der Tod." In *Stücke 3. Die bitteren Tränen der Petra von Kant. Das brennende Dorf. Der Müll, die Stadt und der Tod*. Frankfurt am Main: Suhrkamp, 1976. 91–128.

——. *In einem Jahr mit 13 Monden*. Filmverlag der Autoren, 1978, 2 hr., 4 min.

Finkielkraut, Alain. *Der eingebildete Jude*, Frankfurt am Main: Fischer, 1984.

Frei, Norbert. *Vergangenheitspolitik. Die Anfänge der Bundesrepublik und die NS-Vergangenheit*. Munich: dtv, 2003.

Friedrich, Jörg. *Die kalte Amnestie. NS-Täter in der Bundesrepublik*. Frankfurt am Main: Fischer, 1984.

Funk, Mirna. "Leichenberge, bäm!" *Zeit Online*, January 21, 2017. http://www.zeit.de/freitext/2017/01/21/yolocaust-shahak-shapira-erinnerungskultur/.

Furman, Liliana, and Liliana Ruth Feierstein. "Die Brücke aus Papier: Jüdische Antworten auf die Zerstörung." In *Jüdischer Buchbesitz als Raubgut*. Edited by Regine Dehnel. Frankfurt am Main: Vittorio Klostermann, 2006. 180–82.

Geisel, Eike. "Ende der Schonzeit." *konkret* 5 (1995).

——. *Die Wiedergutwerdung der Deutschen: Essays und Polemiken*. Berlin: Tiamat, 2015.

Giordano, Ralph. *Die zweite Schuld*. Cologne: Kiepenheuer & Witsch, 2015.

Goldmann, Ayala. "Was für ein Symbol." *Jüdische Allgemeine*. July 30, 2015, 3.

Gomringer, Nora. "Und es war ein Tag." *Evangelisch-Lutherischer Sprengel Hildesheim-Göttingen*. April 19, 2012. https://sprengelhildesheimgoettingen.wordpress.com/2012/04/19/auschwitz-gedicht-von-nora-gomringer/ [no longer available].

Grossmann, Atina. "Victims, Villains, and Survivors: Gendered Perceptions and Self-Perceptions of Jewish Displaced Persons in Occupied Postwar Germany." *Journal of the History of Sexuality* 11.1 and 11.2 (2002): 308–10.

Hartewig, Karin. *Zurückgekehrt. Die Geschichte der jüdischen Kommunisten in der DDR*. Cologne: Böhlau Verlag, 2000.

"'Hass-Inhalte'. Kölner Polizei zeigt AfD-Vize von Storch an—Twitter-Account gesperrt." *Berliner Zeitung*. January 1, 2018. https://www.berliner-zeitung.de/politik/-hass-inhalte--koelner-polizei-zeigt-afd-vize-von-storch-an---twitter-account-gesperrt-29417198.

Heine, Heinrich. *Deutschland—Ein Wintermärchen*. Munich: dtv, 1993.

——. *Germany. A Winter's Tale*. Translated by Joseph Massaad. https://www.heinrich-heine.net/winter/wintereng27.htm.

Heym, Stefan. *Ahasver*. Munich: C. Bertelsmann Verlag, 1981.

Höcke, Björn. "Rede zum 3. Kyffhäusertreffen." Der Flügel, filmed September 2, 2017. Video of lecture. http://www.youtube.com/watch?v=7ALZpg3gIGk [no longer available].

"Höcke-Rede im Wortlaut." *Tagesspiegel*, January 19, 2017. https://www.tagesspiegel.de/politik/hoecke-rede-im-wortlaut-gemuetszustand-eines-total-besiegten-volkes/19273518.html.

Jünger, Ernst. "Unsere Politiker." *Die Standarte*. September 6, 1925, 1.

Jureit, Ulrike, and Christian Schneider. *Gefühlte Opfer. Illusionen der Vergangenheitsbewältigung*. Bonn: Klett-Cotta, 2010.

Kahane, Anetta. "Wenn es Antisemitismus nicht geben darf." *Frankfurter Rundschau*. December 18, 2017. http://www.fr.de/politik/meinung/kolumnen/judenfeindlichkeit-wenn-es-antisemitismus-nicht-geben-darf-a-1410085.

Kahn, Daniel, and the Painted Birds. "Six Million Germans / Nakam." Track 6 on *Partisans & Parasites*. Oriente Musik, 2009.

Kamann, Matthias. "AfD ist einer der wenigen Garanten jüdischen Lebens." *welt.de*. April 6, 2017. https://www.welt.de/politik/deutschland/article163446354/AfD-ist-einer-der-wenigen-Garanten-juedischen-Lebens.html. Previously published as "AfD: Politischer Islam ist größte Bedrohung für Demokratie," in *Neue Osnabrücker Zeitung*, April 19, 2016: https://www.presseportal.de/pm/58964/3304772.

"Kanak Attak und Basta!" Kanak Attak. 1998. http://www.kanak-attak.de/ka/archiv/passagiere/manifest/manif_dt.htm.

Kilomba, Grada. *Plantation Memories. Episodes of Everyday Racism*. Münster: Unrast, 2010.

Kiyak, Mely. "Eine Mauer aus Sprachmüll und Politfolklore." Kiyaks Theaterkolumne [blog published by Maxim Gorki Theater, Berlin]. http://kolumne.gorki.de/Kolumne-77/.

Kögel, Annette. "Geb. 1970. Attila Murat Aydin." *tagesspiegel.de*. August 22, 2003. https://www.tagesspiegel.de/berlin/geb-1970/441540.html.

Kolitz, Zvi. *Jossel Rakovers Wendung zu Gott*. Zurich: Diogenes Verlag, 2004.

Kuba, Andreas. *Killing Nazis*. ORF, 2013.

Lagodinsky, Sergey. "Der Morgen und danach . . . Die Suche nach einem neuen politischen Selbstverständnis für die jüdische Gemeinschaft." In: *Ausgerechnet Deutschland!* Edited by Dmitrij Belkin and Raphael Gross. 168–70.

Lang, Berel. "Holocaust Memory and Revenge: The Presence of the Past." *Jewish Social Studies* 2.2 (1996): 1–20.

Leggewie, Claus, and Erik Meyer, *"Ein Ort, an den man gerne geht":* *Das Holocaust-Mahnmal und die Geschichtspolitik nach 1989*. Munich: Hanser, 2005.

Leo, Per, Maximilian Steinbeis, and Daniel-Pascal Zorn. *Mit Rechten reden*. Stuttgart: Klett-Cotta, 2017.

Levi, Primo. *Collected Poems*. Translated by Ruth Feldman and Brian Swann. London: Faber & Faber, 1988.

——. *Wann, wenn nicht jetzt?* Munich: dtv, 1989.

——. *Zu ungewisser Stunde. Gedichte*. Munich and Vienna: Carl Hanser Verlag, 1998.

Lichtenstein, Heiner. *Die Fassbinder-Kontroverse oder Das Ende der Schonzeit*. Bodenheim: Königstein, 1986.

Lichtmesz, Martin, and Caroline Sommerfeld. *Mit Linken leben*, Schnellroda: Verlag Antaios, 2017.

Lohaus, Stefanie, Janne Knödler, and Vina Yun. "'Bist du … ähm … ?' Drei jüdische Feministinnen, zwei volle Aschenbecher, ein Thema: Antisemitismus." *Missy Magazine*. January 29, 2018. https://missy-magazine.de/blog/2018/01/29/bist-du-aehm/.

Lustiger, Arno. *Zum Kampf auf Leben und Tod!* Munich: dtv, 1997.

Maizière, Thomas de. "'Wir sind nicht Burka': De Maizières Thesen zur Leitkultur." *Bild*. May 2, 2017. https://www.bild.de/news/aktuelles/news/wir-sind-nicht-burka-de-maizieres-thesen-51560496.bild.html.

Marx, Karl. *Zur Judenfrage*, Berlin: Rowohlt, 1919.

Messerschmidt, Astrid. "Postkoloniale Erinnerungsprozesse in einer postnationalsozialistischen Gesellschaft—vom Umgang mit Rassismus und Antisemitismus." *Peripherie—Zeitschrift für Politik und Ökonomie in der Dritten Welt* 28.109/110 (2008): 42–60.

"Milliardenüberschuss bei Agentur für Arbeit." *tagesschau.de*. January 11, 2018. https://www.tagesschau.de/wirtschaft/bundesagentur-arbeit-ueberschuss-101.html [no longer available].

"Mitglieder jüdischer Gemeinden in Deutschland 1955–2016." April 25, 2017. https://fowid.de/meldung/mitglieder-juedischer-gemeinden-deutschland-1955-2016.

Mohler, Armin. *Die konservative Revolution in Deutschland 1918–1932. Ein Handbuch*. Graz: Leopold Stocker Verlag, 2005.

Mutlu-Hamaz, Ergün. *Kara Günlük. Die geheimen Tagebücher des Sesperado*. Münster: Unrast, 2012.

"Niedrigster Wert seit der Wiedervereinigung" *tagesschau.de*. January 4, 2018. https://www.tagesschau.de/wirtschaft/ arbeitsmarkt-249.html [no longer available].

Opitz, May, Katharina Oguntoye, and Dagmar Schultz. *Farbe bekennen. Afro-deutsche Frauen auf den Spuren ihrer Geschichte.* Berlin: Orlanda Frauenverlag, 1986.

Peck, Raoul, director. *I Am Not Your Negro.* Magnolia Pictures, 2016, 95 min.

Popp, Maximilian. "Schuld ohne Sühne." *Spiegel Online.* January 20, 2017. http://www.spiegel.de/einestages/tuerkei-die-ermordung-des-journalisten-hrant-dink-2007-a-1130340. html.

Rajber, Roy. "Unser Sommermärchen." *Jüdische Allgemeine.* July 30, 2015, 1.

Reifenberger, Julia. *Girls with Guns. Rape & Revenge Movies: Radikalfeministische Ermächtigungsfantasien?* Berlin: Bertz + Fischer, 2013.

Reschke, Anja. 2018. "Kommentar: Anja Reschke, NDR, zum Gedenken an Auschwitz." *tagesschau.de*. April 21. https:// www.tagesschau.de/multimedia/video/video-58075.html.

Rigoll, Dominik. *Staatsschutz in Westdeutschland: Von der Entnazifizierung zur Extremistenabwehr.* Göttingen: Wallstein Verlag, 2013.

Rommelspacher, Birgit. *Dominanzkultur.* Berlin: Orlanda-Frauenverlag, 1995.

Salamander, Rachel. "Man kann nicht Wurzeln im Nichts schlagen. Rede zur Verleihung des Kulturellen Ehrenpreises der Stadt München." *Frankfurter Allgemeine Zeitung*, January 27, 1999.

Sarrazin, Thilo. *Deutschland schafft sich ab. Wie wir unser Land aufs Spiel setzen*. Munich: Deutsche Verlags-Anstalt, 2010.

Schueler, Hans. "Was hat der Frankfurter Intendant Günther Rühle wirklich gesagt?" *Die Zeit*. December 5, 1986.

Sebald, W. G. *On the Natural History of Destruction*. Translated by Anthea Bell. New York: Random House, 2003.

Shakespeare, William. *The Merchant of Venice*. New York: Simon & Schuster, 2010.

Shapira, Shahak. *Das wird man ja wohl noch schreiben dürfen! Wie ich der deutscheste Jude der Welt wurde*. Reinbek: Rowohlt Taschenbuch, 2016.

—— (@ShahakShapira). "@PostelGert Gert ganz ehrlich der Zug nach Auschwitz holt mich mehr ab als deine Tweets." Twitter, August 30, 2017. https://twitter.com/ShahakShapira/status/902926108953378817.

Shire, Michael. *Die Pessach Haggada*. Berlin: Hentrich & Hentrich Verlag, 2013.

Sieferle, Rolf Peter. *Finis Germania*. Schnellroda: Verlag Antaios, 2017.

Solms-Laubach, Franz. "Seehofer mischt die GroKo auf." *Bild*. March 16, 2018. https://www.bild.de/politik/inland/horst-seehofer/reaktionen-seehofer-55113974.bild.html.

Sow, Noah. *Deutschland Schwarz Weiß. Der alltägliche Rassismus*. Munich: C. Bertelsmann Verlag, 2008.

SpongeBOZZ. "Yellow Bar Mitzvah." Directed by Daniel Zlotin. 2017. Music video, 3:53. https://www.youtube.com/watch?v=C71rzt6FIWI.

Steinmeier, Frank-Walter. "Festakt zum Tag der Deutschen Einheit." October 3, 2017, http://www.bundespraesident.

de/SharedDocs/Reden/DE/Frank-Walter-Steinmeier/
Reden/2017/10/171003-TdDE-Rede-Mainz.html.

Tarantino, Quentin. *Inglourious Basterds: A Screenplay*. New York: Weinstein Books and Little, Brown & Co., 2009.

Tibi, Bassam. *Europa ohne Identität? Die Krise der multikulturellen Gesellschaft*. Munich: Bertelsmann, 1998.

Tobias, Jim G., and Peter Zinke. *Nakam—Jüdische Rache an NS-Tätern*, Hamburg: Konkret Literatur Verlag, 2000.

Treitschke, Heinrich von. "Unsere Aussichten." *Preußische Jahrbücher* 44.5 (November 1879): 572–76.

"Trügerische Erinnerungen: Wie sich Deutschland an die Zeit des Nationalsozialismus erinnert." Presented at Haus der Bundespressekonferenz: Berlin, February 13, 2018. https://www.stiftung-evz.de/fileadmin/user_upload/EVZ_Uploads/Pressemitteilungen/MEMO_PK_final_13.2.pdf [no longer available].

Tucholsky, Kurt. *Deutschland, Deutschland über alles. Ein Bilderbuch*. Berlin: Neuer Deutscher Verlag, 1929.

Utlu, Deniz. "Für Trauer und Zorn. Plädoyer gegen eine Ökonomie des Gedenkens." *Standpunkte* 13 (2013): 4. https://www.rosalux.de/fileadmin/rls_uploads/pdfs/Standpunkte/Standpunkte_13-2013.pdf.

——. "Ins Herz. Wandel einer subversiven Kiezkultur in Berlin." *freitext* 15 (2010): 6–16.

von Waldstein, Thor. *Metapolitik*, Schnellroda: Verlag Antaios, 2015.

von Weizsäcker, Richard. "Gedenkveranstaltung im Plenarsaal des Deutschen Bundestages zum 40. Jahrestag des Endes des Zweiten Weltkrieges in Europa." Deutscher Bundestag, transcribed in Bonn, May 8, 1985. Official translation of speech: https://www.bundespraesident.de/SharedDocs/ Downloads/DE/Reden/2015/02/150202-RvW-Rede-8-Mai-1985-englisch.pdf?__blob=publicationFile.

Walser, Martin. "Dankesrede von Martin Walser zur Verleihung des Friedenspreises des Deutschen Buchhandels in der Frankfurter Paulskirche am 11. Oktober 1998." Börsenverein des Deutschen Buchhandels e. V., filmed October 11, 1998, in Frankfurt am Main. Transcript of speech. https://hdms. bsz-bw.de/files/440/walserRede.pdf.

Wasser, Edgar. "Deutschsein." https://www.youtube.com/watch?v=-Nx3To9q3Hc.

Welzer, Harald, Sabine Moller, and Karoline Tschuggnall. *"Opa war kein Nazi". Nationalsozialismus und Holocaust im Familiengedächtnis*. Frankfurt am Main: Fischer, 2002.

Wieseltier, Leon. "Against Identity." *The New Republic*. November 28, 1994. https://newrepublic.com/article/92857/against-identity.

Wohl, Lea. "'Kommt, lasst uns alle Juden sein!' Jüdische Gegen-Bilder und antisemitische Kommentare auf YouTube." In *Videoportale: Broadcast Yourself? Versprechen und Enttäuschung*. Edited by Julia Schumacher and Andreas Stuhlmann. Hamburg: Hamburger Hefte zur Medienkultur, 2011. 185–95.

Wolf, Christa. *Kindheitsmuster*, Berlin and Weimar: Aufbau Verlag, 1976.

Zick, Andreas, and Jonas Rees. *MEMO Deutschland—Multidimensionaler Erinnerungsmonitor*. Bielefeld: Institut für interdisziplinäre Konflikt- und Gewaltforschung, 2018.

Zwerenz, Gerhard. *Die Erde ist unbewohnbar wie der Mond*. Frankfurt am Main: Fischer, 1973.

DR. MAX CZOLLEK was born in Berlin in 1987, where he attended the Jüdische Oberschule Berlin. He studied Political Science at the Technische Universität Berlin and received his PhD at the Center for Research on Antisemitism. Czollek is the curator of numerous events and festivals on contemporary Jewish culture, and co-editor for the magazine *Jalta—Positionen zur jüdischen Gegenwart* [Yalta—Positions on the Jewish Contemporary]. In addition to *Desintegriert Euch!* (Hanser, 2018) and *Gegenwartsbewältigung* (Hanser, 2020), he is the author of three volumes of poetry published by Verlagshaus Berlin: *Druckkammern* (2012), *Jubeljahre* (2015), and *Grenzwerte* (2019). He lives and writes in Berlin.

DR. JON CHO-POLIZZI is an educator, activist, and freelance literary translator, and a Collegiate Fellow and Assistant Professor of German at the University of Michigan. Cho-Polizzi received his PhD in German and Medieval Studies from UC Berkeley after studying Translation, History, and Literature in Heidelberg and Santa Cruz. He lives and works between Ann Arbor, Northern California, and Berlin.

RESTLESS BOOKS is an independent, nonprofit publisher devoted to championing essential voices from around the world whose stories speak to us across linguistic and cultural borders. We seek extraordinary international literature for adults and young readers that feeds our restlessness: our hunger for new perspectives, passion for other cultures and languages, and eagerness to explore beyond the confines of the familiar.

Through cultural programming, we aim to celebrate immigrant writing and bring literature to underserved communities. We believe that immigrant stories are a vital component of our cultural consciousness; they help to ensure awareness of our communities, build empathy for our neighbors, and strengthen our democracy.

Visit us at www.restlessbooks.org